Horse Camping

Horse Camping

by George B. Hatley

photographs by Lewis Portnoy
foreword by Juli S. Thorson

Washington State University Press
Pullman, Washington

Washington State University Press
PO Box 645910
Pullman, Washington 99164-5910
Phone: 800-354-7360
Fax: 509-335-8568
E-mail: wsupress@wsu.edu
Web site: wsupress.wsu.edu

Originally published by Dial Press 1981

Library of Congress Cataloging-in-Publication Data

Hatley, George B., 1924-
  Horse camping / George B. Hatley ; photographs by Lewis Portnoy ;
foreword by Juli S. Thorson.
      p. cm.
  Originally published: New York : Dial Press, c1981.
  Includes bibliographical references.
  ISBN 978-0-87422-303-3 (alk. paper)
  1. Packhorse camping. I. Portnoy, Lewis. II. Title.
  GV199.62.H37 2009
  796.54--dc22
                                    2009045891

Fine Quality Books from the Pacific Northwest

CONTENTS

FOREWORD TO THE REVISED EDITION

A S A GIRL GROWING UP in the flat farming country of North Dakota, I dreamed of riding mountain trails and taking horse-camping trips with George Hatley long before I met him. His articles on these activities appeared regularly in such publications as *Western Horseman* and *Appaloosa News*, two magazines that were staples in our home in the 1960s and '70s. Many of George's first-hand tales were of taking guests out into backcountry areas he'd explored since boyhood, and I coveted these campfire companions their luck at being invited.

Little did I know that I would one day be granted just that brand of luck. New journalism degree in hand, I wrote to George—an icon I'd never met—to ask for a job at the horse magazine he oversaw out west in Moscow, Idaho. He hired me, then befriended me, and despite cringing over some of my flatlander ways with horses, he also added me to his riding-partner guest list.

This explains, in part, my original involvement with this book. I was among the party assembled for the trip taken to produce the book's photos (and appear, looking 30 years younger, as the beaming gal with the curly brown hair).

Even as our group of seven shopped and chose gear for our George Hatley-led trip into Idaho's remote and rugged Seven Devils mountains, I had the eerily prescient conviction that I was about to embark on what would someday stand as the adventure of a lifetime. The ensuing years have proven this true—at least, so far!

Part of what made the trip so grand was knowing we were in the utmost of capable hands. When it comes to earned experience out on the trail with horses, George is the real

deal. All of us, seasoned riders and greenhorns alike, were confident we could put our full trust in George to get us into the wild without mishap and bring us back out in one piece. He delivered on that front—no small feat in itself, considering the terrain, range of rider skill, and the sole responsibility for nearly a dozen head of stock. One seldom has opportunity to be included in the immediate sphere of someone so competent.

George's knowledge of Northwest history, flora and fauna also helped make our sojourn significant. When one rides into new country, it's natural to be curious about its past and its living present. Thanks to the lifelong student who led our way on this trip, we did not go lacking in that area.

Nor did we go hungry for tasty meals— "grub," in our host's parlance. Using nothing more sophisticated than campfire cooking gear, George fed us well from, among other resources, the tried-and-true recipes included in this book.

All this is by way of assuring you that you can rely on the horse-camping guidance to be found on subsequent pages. And don't let the passage of time lead you to believe that George's advice is obsolete. While trucks and trailers may be more modernized, and although high-tech options are now available for camping outwear and the like, the basics of horse camping, the nature of horses, and the soul satisfactions of getting out and beyond remain unchanged from the days of the first mountain men—and earlier.

Just as important, a horseback trip out into remote country promises to be even more restorative to today's would-be adventurer than our trip with George was three decades ago. In our contemporary times, we are blessed, yet somehow trapped, by the digital revolution that makes so much of life "virtual" rather than truly experiential. Horse camping offers the perfect antidote. It allows you—make that *requires* you—to see the non-virtual world again with the freshest of eyes, because it rivets your attention and all your senses to the *now*.

I've ridden into many camps on many horses since following George Hatley's lead into the Seven Devils in 1981, and have employed slices of his expertise each time. There's just no other experience quite like horse camping, and no one more able to teach you its ropes than the man who wrote this book.

Juli S. Thorson
Moscow, Idaho
September 2009

ACKNOWLEDGMENTS FROM THE ORIGINAL EDITION

Many people contribute to a book. Some stimulate interest and incentive, some provide information, and others do the time-consuming work such as typing the manuscript.

My first interest was kindled by stories of my grandfather, Riley B. Hatley, who came west when the plains were still alive with buffalo. The enthusiasm of the late G. J. Tucker, who worked as a district ranger during the horse-packing era of the United States Forest Service, sparked incentive.

Learning to pack (without a book) came from piecing together small bits of information from experienced people. Among those who taught me, and who have ridden over the last divide, are Lewis G. Ferguson, Neil Hatley, and Wallace Espy.

Earl Hibbs had a wealth of packing knowledge to share because he started packing at the age of eight. Lee Manes, who started professional packing in 1934, was a good teacher. Other packers who shared their skills were Jess Earl, Larry Gardner, Dick Hammond, Roy Tumelson, Lloyd Jones, Jack Nygaard, and Bill Sullivan.

Ester Hibbs helped greatly with the food and cooking sections. She had gained a wealth of experience from spending summers trailing the cattle to summer range, camping with them, and then returning them to winter range in the fall.

The photographer, Lewis Portnoy, worked hard to get the best-ever horse camping pictures for this book. He was intent on getting the pictures, yet was a pleasure to work with. Other members of the photographic party were Juli Thorson, Dorothy MacEachern, Suzie Gulick, Kris Portnoy, and Terry Lawhead. They

all pitched in, and seemed to have as much fun when they worked as when they played.

Kode Parkins (age six) rode her horse for the photographer and proved she was qualified to go horse camping. Juli Thorson, who teaches publications editing at the University of Idaho, helped as the book was being written. Margie Berndt lent her knowledge of horse trailering. Art Yadon supplied names and addresses of outfitter and guide associations. Carol Escapule was helpful in the spelling and grammar department.

The biggest chore, that of typing the manuscript, was done by Iola Hatley (Mrs. G.B.). She likes horses, but would rather have her horses carrying a jockey to the winner's circle than carrying a camper to some remote mountain lake. She deserves much credit for being tolerant of the time I spend horse camping.

G.B.H.

INTRODUCTION

"YOU CAN SEE WHAT MAN MADE from the seat of an automobile, but the best way to see what God made is from the back of a horse." Thus spoke western artist Charles M. Russell, a do-it-yourself horse camper who deeply loved riding the backcountry.

The appeal of horse camping is deeply rooted. This urge to return to an outdoor life in a primitive setting may be inherited from a time when man was a nomad and camping was the only way of life. Horse camping as we know it today began with hunters and trappers on the North American frontier. While their purpose was harvesting meat and furs, we know from their journals that they enjoyed the country and the camp life. These nineteenth-century mountain men lamented the passing of their way of life, and many stayed in the West to become guides and Army scouts.

It was the glowing accounts of the mountain men that attracted sportsmen who were willing to pay outfitters and guides to help them enjoy the wilderness. Sir William Stewart, Grand Duke Alexis, and Teddy Roosevelt all retained professional guides on their camping expeditions. As soon as these first "dudes" let others know the joys of horse camping, the outfitting business grew rapidly.

A major impetus to horse camping was the establishment of a professional service at the beginning of the twentieth century to watch over the forests as a national resource. For many years, U.S. Forest Service personnel were busy cutting trails and building lookout towers on the higher peaks. The only way to take materials and supplies into the backwoods was on the back of horses and mules, and thousands of miles of trails were built and used for that purpose. Fortunately for us, these trails and campsites have been left for us to use for recreation.

Horse camping can be one of life's special experiences. As my friend Snowden Carter described his first pack trip: "I was feeling so good I could hardly stand it. Unreal. A dream. What had happened to the rest of the world? At that moment, it didn't matter. Here, at last, was the complete bliss so frequently sought and so seldom attained."

By going into the backcountry on a horse, the camper doesn't have to make a packhorse out of himself, and his feet don't ache. Horses also make the outdoors accessible to people who are incapable of hiking, such as the very young, the very old, amputees, diabetics, and heart patients.

In many parks and wilderness areas, the country near to the roads is overused and the remote portions are almost unused. Horses get people into the unused areas. The horse gives you the carrying capacity to help others.

Since 1955, the horse population in the United States has increased from 4.5 million to over 9 million. There are many useable horses. There are many owners who would like to go horse camping, but don't know how. This book tells how.

George B. Hatley
Alpowa Ranch, Washington
May 1981

1. Planning

CRESTING THE HIGH RIDGE and looking suddenly down on Ship Island Lake caused me to rein in. I felt that I needed to get to solid ground and hang on to the nearest tree—this was too dramatic a scene to absorb from a moving horse.

Ship Island, with masts of tall spruce, stood moored with its shimmering lake harbor below. A ridge of organ pipe spires rose on the left, and on the right was a sheer mountain face plunging straight to the shore. Beyond lay the canyon of the Middle Fork of the Salmon River, while mountains, like white-crested waves, reached to the horizon.

Horse camping takes the rider to the spectacular and the unspoiled, but not without planning. Years ago, my uncle, Norman Hatley, was planning a pack trip to entertain his son-in-law and three other guests from Washington, D.C. None of the four had ever been horse camping. Norman's original plan was to take them over the Seven Devils and down into Hells Canyon, but when he called the ranger station, he learned the trail was still blocked by snow, as it usually is until after the Fourth of July.

Norman could have taken the party up the Snake River trail from Pittsburg Landing to Hells Canyon where the elevation is low and weather is good in June. He knew the trail and the good places to camp, and could have shown his guests some beautiful country. But as he also wanted to see some new territory, Norman decided to take the group to Maude and Lotte Lakes in the Selway-Bitterroot Wilderness.

Packing into such a high area in June can be a risk, but the trail was clear and the group enjoyed packing in. They were blessed with one day of good fishing before it began to snow. The fish continued to bite, but fishing in the snow loses its appeal, particularly when you are dressed for June in Washington, D.C. After the third day of snow, everyone agreed to pack out. The melting snow made the trail slick and, as Norman said, "I came off the mountain with four very blue bureaucrats."

All did not end badly. The party moved to Norman's cow camp, rode out to streams within comfortable distance of camp, and enjoyed the remainder of their vacation in mild weather with good fishing.

Think ahead. Plan your time and mileage in order to get into camp well before dark. It is much easier to set up camp in the daylight, and it is far easier on the riders to have a short day in the saddle.

I once passed up a good campsite about five o'clock in the afternoon and continued on for another three hours to the next camp. My guests were exhausted and we faced unpacking and setting up camp in the dark—a time-consuming, difficult task. Fortunately, an outfitter, Jack Nygaard, and his family were camped nearby. Jack came over and invited my guests to his fire while he helped me unpack and set up camp.

I've learned that everything about a horse camping trip, including planning, takes a little more time than I anticipate. By allowing more time, and not attempting to go too far or too fast, the trip takes on a relaxed, happy, under-control atmosphere.

PLACE

Horse camping can be done anywhere on the North American continent where it is legal to take horses and where the climate and terrain make horse camping pleasant for both camper and horse. For example the Appaloosa Horse Club has an annual five-day ride in Kentucky's Daniel Boone National Forest. Most horse camping is done in the West, but there are good horse camping locations in every state and province.

Much public land is open for horse camping. Some is not, and for that reason, always contact the land manager of the area under consideration and ask if horses can be used.

Private landowners occasionally make their property available for horse camping, but many have stopped the practice after careless campers abused the privilege.

Uninvited guests trespassing on private land are too often careless about leaving litter and closing gates. These are the two most common complaints cited by private owners for keeping their land closed. Users of both public and private land must recognize that access is a privilege, not a right. The land must be treated with the same respect as one's own front yard.

A wide variety of country can be reached by pack string. There is sharp contrast between the Arizona desert with its giant saguaro cactus and the Canadian Rockies with their towering snow-covered peaks and rushing streams.

Choosing the place for your trip depends upon what you want to see, do, or investigate.

Whether your aim is fishing, scenery, or old mining towns, keep in mind the characteristics of a good horse camping area. Well-marked and maintained trails are important. You will need drinking water for both people and horses, and good grazing for the horses. In the beginning, avoid steep, rugged, rocky country, and choose terrain where horse and rider will both be comfortable. If you are limited by time, look for a place where the trailhead can be reached in one day to simplify hauling—although there are horse motels along most major interstates in the western United States. An internet search for 'horse motel' will yield places that offer overnight lodging for horses.

TIME

THE TIME TO TAKE a pack trip depends on such factors as geographic location, weather, fishing or hunting seasons, insects, trail maintenance, and graze. First decide where to go, and then find out when that place offers the best combination of desirable factors.

February and March are good months in the southern tier of states and in Mexico, but are miserable, if not impossible, for camping in the northern states and Canada. Mid-August is usually a good time to pack into high mountain country of Canada and Alaska and into the Rocky Mountain, Bitterroot, Cascade, and Sierra ranges of the lower forty-eight states.

In mountainous areas, weather varies greatly with altitude. Some high mountain trails will be blocked by snow until the first part of August. Even when care is taken to determine the optimum time to travel, you are still at the mercy of erratic weather conditions in any mountainous area.

On a pack trip into the Bighorn Crags of Idaho, it snowed six inches on the fifteenth of August. The purpose of the trip was to film a travelogue-type movie of horse camping in an unusually scenic area. The unplanned snow was certainly scenic, but it also collapsed one tent and considerably dampened the enthusiasm of the movie crew.

The hunting and fishing seasons set by state and provincial game departments will dictate the time when trips after wild game will be made. For the comfort of both you and your horse, you may want to camp when annoying insects, particularly mosquitoes and deer flies, are in abeyance. The further north you go,

however, the insects are at their worst when the weather is at its best. Then, the only solution is plenty of insect repellent.

If you are a beginner, it might be advisable to go later in the season after the trail has been opened by more experienced riders. Long-time horse packers take pride in maintaining the trail as they go along and are equipped to do so with an ax, saw, and shovel.

During unusually dry summers, certain public lands are closed to all types of camping because of fire hazard. Such areas are well publicized and obviously should be avoided.

The time of the year chosen for the trip also depends upon whether or not you are going to graze your horses. The very young, tender grass of early spring is not as abundant or nutritious as mature grass, and close, continuous grazing of such young grass can damage the stand.

INFORMATION

WHILE SOME INFORMATION about a specific area can be obtained from magazine articles and books, the best sources are the land administrators and horse packers who know the area.

Some areas require a permit. When applying for one, it is necessary to list the size of the party, the number of horses being used, and the number of days planned for the trip. Some places have grazing regulations, and others require that all the horse feed be packed in.

Ask an experienced camper about the condition of the trail. Find out if the trail is maintained, and if it is wide, narrow, steep, rocky, or boggy. Ask about overgrown brush and fallen timber. Find out if the trail is easy to follow and is well marked. Ask about places where it would be easy to follow the wrong fork. The type of traffic on the trail is also important—trail bikes, for example, may startle a horse.

Riders who have gone over the trail before can tell you about places to camp that have water, fuel, and grass. Poisonous snakes, poison ivy and oak, and masses of insects can also be avoided by checking beforehand.

Mark your map with directions, and indicate any side trips people might recommend for historic or scenic interest. Determine the location of the nearest telephone (or if there is cellular phone service available), medical doctor, and health care services. This is the type of information you need and hope you never use.

LENGTH

IT IS IMPORTANT to have the trip long enough to be worthwhile, yet not so long as to become an endurance test. A popular trip length uses one weekend to get to the trailhead, includes a week of horse camping, and then uses the following weekend to return home.

The shortest pack trip I recall is one where a party of five wanted to pack into a lake in the Bitterroots over a three-day weekend. I gathered the horses and assembled the pack and riding gear on Thursday afternoon. The others gathered their gear and food together on Thursday evening, and I cargoed it. Friday morning I saddled, loaded, and trucked the six saddle horses and three packhorses 140 miles to the trailhead.

The party arrived at the trailhead at 11 a.m. By noon the horses were packed, and everyone had eaten lunch, filled saddlebags with incidentals, tied his coat and slicker to his saddle, and was ready to go. At the usual pack string rate of three to three-and-one-half miles per hour, the twelve-mile trip took about four hours, and we arrived at the lake well before dark.

Saturday was spent fishing, picking huckleberries to mix in Sunday morning pancakes, and riding out to look at mountain goats. After Sunday breakfast, we packed up, packed out, and were home before evening. Everyone was back at work on Monday morning. It was the first horse camping experience for four of the five, and they were all chomping at the bit to go again when they could spend more time.

The longest pack trips, lasting up to a month, are taken in northern California and Alaska, where outfitters take clients into very remote areas in pursuit of wild game or beautiful scenery. The most popular pack trip lasts five to ten days. A group setting out for its first go at horse camping should try a short trip rather than a long one. After the first few trips, novice horse campers begin to gain skill and confidence, and will enjoy longer trips.

I would rather have my companions complain because the trip was too short than wish it had ended a day earlier. The pace of the trip should be geared to the desire of the party and capability of the horses. Regardless of the route taken, plan out the daily mileage in such a way that neither the riders nor the horses are overworked.

ROUTE

THE POINT OF HORSE CAMPING is to enjoy the country, the ride, the camping, and the people in the party—not to get the mail through to San Francisco before the Overland Express. I recommend a leisurely pace. You can plan on making two-and-one-half to three-and-one half miles an hour with a pack string, depending upon how steep and rocky the trail is. Locate a camping spot well before dark. This gives adequate time to set up camp and give the horses a bite to eat.

For the first trip or two, it is smart to pack into a good campsite, set up camp, and take short day-rides out of that camp. The trip is more relaxing if you do not have to pack up every morning and unpack every evening. The camp will become home, and the horses will adapt to their location. Areas with varying, gentle terrain and a number of trails are best suited for this cloverleaf plan.

With more experienced riders and horses, it is more adventurous to take a circular route. Camp is moved every day or two as you complete the circle. Make certain that you allot time enough to cover the route without the trip becoming a marathon. If time is limited, keep the circle small. It is usually possible to map out a circle, which provides a wide variety of scenery, new places to fish, and adequate grazing for the horses.

The final alternative is to start and finish at separate points, with a distance of 40 to 60 miles between trailhead and trail end. Following a marked trail, such as the Pacific Crest, Continental Divide, or Appalachian, would involve starting at one point and ending at another.

Since 1965, the Appaloosa Horse Club has sponsored the Chief Joseph Trail Ride, an annual ride that each year covers 100 miles of the route taken by the Nez Perce Indians during the 1877 Nez Perce War. The day before the ride begins, everyone takes his horse to the trailhead, then drives his vehicle to the termination camp, parks, and returns to the assembly camp on chartered buses. A camp crew meets the ride each evening with baggage and cook trucks.

Since the sleeping and eating equipment is not carried on pack stock, the ride averages about five miles an hour and covers around twenty miles each day.

PARTY

THE SIZE OF THE PRIVATE horse camping party will first be limited by the number of horses available and your capacity to get them to the trailhead. If a four-horse trailer and four horses are available, a party of two can go camping in luxury, or a party of three could go taking the bare necessities, carrying some gear on the riding horses. If two four-horse trailers and eight horses are available, a party of five can go first class.

I find that a group of four to six people is the best size for most horse camping trips. This is not a burdensome number to cook for, and there are enough people to share the work that must be done. Most camping spots have enough level space for that number and the horses required will not need an excessive amount of forage. If a party is going to high altitude lakes with limited or no grazing, it will be necessary to pack in pelletized horse feed, which

in turn will restrict the size of the group in relation to the number of horses.

Some professional outfitters take much larger parties, depending upon the area, the outfitter, and the wishes of the campers. Pack trips organized by private outfitters take from 2 to 25 people. Rides without pack stock, such as the Chief Joseph Trail Ride mentioned earlier or the Alamo Trail Ride in Texas, will accommodate up to 300 people.

I have taken people horse camping from all walks of life and from the bottom to the top rungs of the socio-economic ladder. The only prerequisites for fitting into a party seem to be an appreciation of nature and a willingness to share the work. It helps if the camper enjoys horses and has an interest in history. Fortunately, horse camping seems to bring out the best in people—no one wants to act ugly in such beautiful surroundings.

OUTFITTERS

OUTFITTERS ARE EXPERIENCED horse handlers who take people horse camping for a fee. They provide a valuable service because they make horse camping possible for many people who would never have the opportunity to outfit themselves.

Outfitting is a very old profession and probably started soon after horses were domesticated. The type of outfitting we know today was well established in the middle of the nineteenth century. Word had gotten out that there was a vast mount of scenic country from Canada down through Mexico, and people who wanted to see it needed transportation, since railroads had not crossed the West and the automobile and the airplane were yet to be developed. Horses provided the way. People enjoyed the experience so much that they kept right on riding into the backcountry even after the automobile came along.

Most present-day outfitters supply everything but a sleeping bag and toothbrush. They have the saddle horses, packhorses or mules, pack outfits, cooking equipment, food, tents, equipment to transport horses to the trailhead, and the necessary personnel to take very good care of the horse camper.

Going with an outfitter provides the ultimate in freedom from work, worry, and responsibility. The outfitter is not learning to pack—he already knows how. He knows the best places to camp, the most scenic places to visit, the hideouts of fish and game, and the location of ghost towns and miners' cabins. He is a part of the Old West still doing business.

Most western states and provinces have outfitter and guide associations (see Sources at the back of this book) which publish lists of outfitters. Armed with such a list, you can contact individual outfitters regarding their services, including the places they pack, the length of their trips, and the cost.

Once you have settled on an outfitter as the way to go, ask him what you are expected to bring in the way of sleeping gear. If a member of the party has a heart or respiratory problem, ask about maximum altitude reached on the trip. You might want to know how long you will be in the saddle, and how much duffle (including your sleeping bag) you are allowed to bring. This is often limited to forty pounds.

The disreputable outfitter is a rare bird. Thieves are lazy, and outfitting requires a lot of work. A majority of outfitters take pride in their profession and try hard to give clients their money's worth. There is a wide variation in the areas where outfitters operate and in the size and quality of their operations. Their most effective advertising is by word of mouth. Having satisfied customers saying good things about them assures a full book for the coming season.

After you've contacted outfitters in the area of your choice, compare their responses and/or brochures. What do their facilities look like? Are people having a good time? Find out what you get for your money. Ask for references. Call or write past clients and ask if the outfitter you are considering offers the type of horse camping you are looking for.

Like most things that are purchased, you generally get what you pay for. Luxury and frills will increase the cost, while the primitive and basic will cost less.

The late Wallace (Fat) Espy was an outfitter. During elk season late one October in the fifties,

I was busy unloading elk meat when a hunter rushed up and said that one of his party was drowning in the river. He had fallen off a raft. I swam across the Lochsa and pulled him out, but he didn't respond to the artificial respiration, having been in the ice-cold water too long to survive. Fat, who was camped nearby, realized that I might succumb to the same fate, and he sent his son Buck across the river at a ford with two saddle horses and my clothes. He took me to his cook tent, thawed me out, fed me, and had me spend the night. Outfitters are a helpful breed of people.

To most outfitters, packing is a way of life. They enjoy the heritage, the country, the stock, and the people. They are unwilling to trade that for an easier, more lucrative pursuit.

IN SHAPE

BEING IN SHAPE for horse camping can make the difference between joy and pain. Saddling horses, cargoing, packing, and setting up camp take some effort. If it weren't fun, it would be work. For two or three weeks before the trip, do some walking, swimming, or jogging. Climb stairs and do some exercises. Sitting at a desk and picking up a pen or a telephone a few times a day does not put a person in shape for anything. If a person gets considerable exercise as part of his work, that should be enough.

Riding uses some muscles and articulates the joints. The pleasure horse owner who rides regularly has no problem. Anyone else needs to cultivate a friend with a horse, or should go to a stable and spend a little time riding. Start slowly and increase the amount of time spent on the horse. Ride an hour every few days until stiffness and soreness disappear. Then, when you can ride for two or three hours without discomfort, you are ready to go horse camping.

CHILDREN

CHILDREN OFTEN cannot tolerate the vacations their parents plan, or are not even welcome on them. Parents who do want to take their children along may be frustrated trying to find some activity everyone can do together—and enjoy. Horse camping is such an activity. Children over the age of two have an amazing capacity to both accept and enjoy horse camping.

I once took a young attorney friend from Tulsa, his wife, and six sons, aged two through twelve, on a pack trip. Even though it was midsummer, it rained, and that often dampens campers' spirits. Despite the adverse weather, the father claims that the vacation was the most memorable family trip they ever took. "The two-year-old doesn't remember much about it, but all the others talk more about the pack trip than anything else we have ever done together," he said.

As adaptable as children are, think twice about a taking a child under two years of age. Unless the child is old enough to sit up unaided, there is no safe way to carry him. The baby boards used by nomadic Indians are no longer available, and trying to ride a horse with a baby in a backpack is dangerous. A very young child also needs special food, including milk, which perishes quickly.

If a small child does become a member of your party, plan for his comfort. Rest stops should be more frequent, especially for a child only recently toilet trained. If the child is still in diapers, take a few more than you think you'll need, and plan to pack the soiled ones out. Take extra changes of clothing, and be sure to take a sunbonnet and sunscreen to protect the child's tender skin.

A child will be most comfortable riding in a child-sized saddle. His seat will be more secure, and the stirrups can be raised high enough to fit. Very small children will usually ride behind or in front of an adult. Young children cannot wait as long between meals as adults, so plan to carry snacks, such as fruit, canned juice, or crackers, in your saddlebag.

Horse camping is a tremendous learning experience for children—they see, hear, and investigate so many new things. Suzie Gulick, age twelve, appears in some of the photographs in this book. She knew how to ride and how to camp, but had never been horse camping. Of the six people on the trip, she probably had a stronger yen to go than anyone. She was an enthusiastic, even exuberant, participant. "That pack trip has been all Suzie can talk about this summer," her mother said.

ELDERS

Horse camping allows the elderly to enjoy the wilderness as much as anyone else. Long after a person is too old to carry a pack and hike into the mountains, he can mount a gentle horse and ride in.

My father went on two pack trips during his 79th year and thoroughly enjoyed every minute. While riding the trail, he did not require any more rest stops than would be taken with a group of young people. If he had any fault, it was setting too fast a pace so he could hurry up and see what was over the next ridge or around the next bend.

If people along in years do require a slower pace or an extra rest stop, it is time well spent for everyone. Older people do not require much extra effort (perhaps an additional foam pad to make each night's sleep more comfortable), but in my experience, the little extra effort of taking older people into the backcountry is worth it.

GOING ALONE

GOING ALONE is a rewarding and exciting experience for some people, but such a person should be a very knowledgeable and self-sufficient horse camper. They must be certain that the rewards are worth the very real risks. If an accident occurs, making contact with the outside world may be impossible.

But risk taking is one of the things that make solo trips a unique experience. The horse camper going alone feels a keenness to do everything correctly and safely, knowing that a mistake could result in a lot of suffering, or even death. Being solely responsible for your own wellbeing and that of your horses in rugged country miles from the nearest person induces an alertness and stimulation that takes a long time to wear off.

Some years ago I drew a mountain sheep permit on the west side of the Middle Fork of the Salmon River. I loaded a saddle horse and two pack-horses in a four-horse trailer and spent the day driving to Big Creek. It was a two-day pack to the mouth of Survey Creek, where I forded the Middle Fork and set up camp. Sheep hunting takes place in very steep and rocky country, and a hunter must take care not to fall. I kept two horses tied while the third grazed, for this is no place to be left afoot. I did not find a three-quarter curl ram, but the trip was one of the most personally rewarding I've ever taken.

If you go alone, make certain that you map out a schedule and stick with it. Give a copy to some friend or relative who is equipped and willing to come looking for you if you fail to return on schedule. Take every care not to foul up.

2. Horses

HORSE CAMPERS ENJOY the role their horses play. The horse is not only a means of getting campers into the wilderness, but is also a partner in an adventure. Part of the excitement is our awareness that the partnership of man and horse goes back to the earliest times.

Great kings, emperors, explorers, and generals were mounted men. Early on, the horse became a symbol of leadership, prestige, and power. The use of the horse in racing, hunting, the Olympic games, and polo contributed to this aura. In North America, mounted Indians, Pony Express riders, mountain men, frontier outlaws, and cowboys all used horses in exciting and daring ways.

For many actual and nostalgic reasons, the horse provides a deep-seated sense of pride, stimulation, and fulfillment. These feelings are heightened on a horse camping trip because the rush and distractions of modern living are shut out. The bond between horse and rider is strengthened because their dependence upon each other is greater.

People have always taken pride and pleasure in owning and using good horses. Having a well-trained horse of good disposition greatly adds to the enjoyment and comfort of a horse trip.

During recent years, competition at horse shows and other equine events has become so keen that many horse owners have turned from participating to spectating. In compensation, they have begun to ride their horses in natural environments. Instead of emphasizing sleekness, pretty heads, thin necks, fox ears, and tiny feet, these horse owners have learned to appreciate horses that are easy to ride, sure-footed, and trail-wise.

A majority of horses today are overfed and underused. Horses are capable of doing more work than people realize. My dad thought that horses were put here for the convenience of man rather than man for the convenience of horses. He did not abuse horses, but he felt that they should work for a living. If a former show horse is going to be used on tail rides or pack trips, it should be fed less and exercised more to keep its weight down and to build wind.

I knew one woman who had accepted riding one of her ex-show horses on the trail, but considered packing it beneath the beast's dignity. Not so. It is no disgrace for a horse to carry a pack rather than a person. Of the fifteen geldings and two mares that I use on the ranch and on pack trips, all have been ridden and all have been packed. Some are better for riding and others for packing, but they are all useable in either capacity.

From a low point of 4.5 million horses in 1955, the horse population in the United States has expanded to more than 9 million today. Many people who have been hauling horses to a show each weekend are not thinking in terms of letting the horses haul them into some good horse camping country. With gasoline prices what they are, horses hauling people makes more sense than people hauling horses.

Saddle Horses

Saddle horses that will be used by a beginner for horse camping will usually be the horses he presently owns, or horses owned by a friend or an outfitter. The majority will be pleasure horses, while others will be ranch horses, show horses, or hunters. The pleasure horse that gets considerable riding does very well on a pack trip because it has been exposed to dogs, ditches, motorcycles, and a wide variety of sights and sounds. Horses used for ranch work are ideal for horse camping.

Show horses have one advantage. Because they have been hauled thousands of miles, they load easily and haul well. The pack trip will expose them to many unfamiliar things. Some of these horses will spook and shy while others will just stop in their tracks until they get accustomed to passing odd-shaped boulders and tree stumps that look like alligators. They will get through the trip, but slowly, which isn't such a great disadvantage. Hunting horses do very well horse camping because they have already been exposed to about everything they will see on a pack trip. Hunters are athletes, and a pack trip will be less effort than a fox hunt.

The Bureau of Land Management occasionally puts out "wild horses" for adoption. If and when the new owners get these horses broken, they would be useable for horse trips. Don't let them loose to graze, because you may never see them again.

If you are going on a pack trip with an outfitter, tell him exactly how much riding experience you have had and let him select your mount. The horse that looks the prettiest might not give you the safest and most comfortable ride. The outfitter knows his horses' training, riding qualities, and dispositions. He has also had experience in matching the rider with the right horse.

PACKHORSES

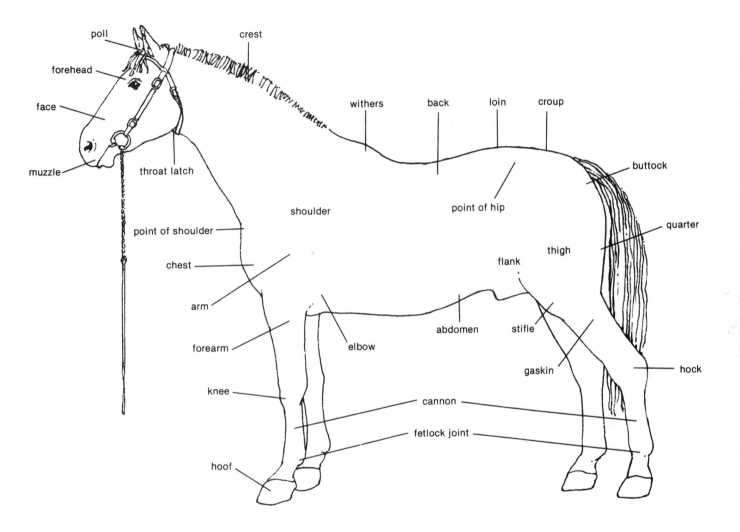

poll — forehead — face — muzzle — throat latch — crest — withers — back — loin — croup — buttock — quarter — point of shoulder — shoulder — point of hip — thigh — flank — chest — arm — abdomen — stifle — forearm — elbow — gaskin — hock — knee — cannon — fetlock joint — hoof

ANY SADDLE HORSE can be used as a pack-horse. A horse becomes a packhorse by being packed. Until the horse becomes familiar with it, it may resent the breeching of the packsaddle. If a horse is being packed for the first time, get it used to both the saddle and the packing before you start the trip. A packhorse needs to lead well and be willing to cross creeks, rocks, and logs. It needs to be tolerant of the horse it is following and the horse behind it.

Strange horses can take a dislike to one another. Often they will get over their anti-social behavior if given a chance to become acquainted. If horses from different strings are going to be taken on a trip together, one way to promote horse harmony is to turn them loose in a pasture together for a week or two before the trip. If this cannot be done, extra care should be taken to hook together packhorses that will get along, or to split the group up into short strings.

Horses taken on a pack trip should be easy to catch.

SIZE AND SHAPE

If you have a choice, avoid using a low or sheep-withered horse. If you have to ride one, use a breeching or crupper. If you have to pack such a horse, have the load perfectly balanced, packed low, and cinched tight.

Excessive width is also a disadvantage if the country is steep and the trails are narrow. A very wide horse is harder to ride and will shake his rider or cargo more than a narrow horse. A wide horse is more subject to stumbling on steep ground. A horse that is two feet wide between the front legs will have trouble on a trail that is only one foot wide. Considering the excessive width of some horses, it is a good thing that most trails are two or three feet wide.

A horse with very straight hind legs will shake you or the cargo going downhill. One that is just a little sickle-hocked will let you go down easier than a horse that is too straight.

Avoid horses with offset knees and calf knees. If its pasterns are short and straight, a horse will give a jarring ride. If they are too long and sloping, the pasterns will be too weak for heavy loads, which could injure the fetlock area.

Foot size should be in proportion to the horse, or even somewhat large. A horse with very small feet carries too much weight on too little bearing surface, and is much more subject to foot problems such as navicular disease. Small feet will tend to sink into soft or boggy ground. This is particularly important in northern Canada and Alaska where there are long stretches of soft muskeg.

A very thin-skinned horse with short, fine hair will be more apt to get scratched, and will suffer more from insects and cold nights. As it turns out, many of the qualities desirable in show horses are less useful or detrimental in horses used on pack trips.

HORSES OF NEARLY EVERY SIZE and shape have been ridden and packed. A very tall horse will cause you to lose your hat on overhanging limbs and is more difficult to pack or mount. A short horse will get your feet wet when you ford a stream. Largeness does not necessarily mean superior capacity to get across the country. Most of the winning endurance horses, the ones that cover one hundred miles in fourteen hours or fifty miles in three-and-one-half hours, are often small and a little on the narrow side. But they are deep through the heart girth, from withers to underline.

The shape of the horse's back is very important both for riding in mountains and for packing. Well-defined, prominent withers are most helpful in keeping both riding saddles and packsaddles in place. Unfortunately, too many horse show judges have overlooked the importance of withers, and because of their indifference, too many horse breeders have neglected this area.

TRAINING

A SADDLE HORSE REQUIRES little training to prepare it for horse camping. It should be receptive to being mounted on either side and to leading another horse or string of horses. The more exposure a horse has to unusual sights and sounds, the less it will be disturbed by the new world it encounters on a pack trip. In truth, the only way a horse gets "trained" for horse camping is by going camping. The horse will soon accept the new life. Some horses seem to take to it with the same enthusiasm they have when turned out into a fresh new pasture in the spring.

The packhorse must be trained to stand quietly while being packed. If there are problems, and you are unsure how to handle them, get experienced help. Then, if the horse wants to move around, hobble it. If it refuses to be packed, tie up a hind leg. A horse frightened by the pack can be blindfolded until the pack is securely tied on. If the horse wants to buck, an experienced hand can fasten a heavy wire to the right side of the front fork, bring it around the horse's neck so it is snug and wrap it securely to the left side of the fork. Then, when the horse tries to put its head down to buck, its air will be cut off. In the long run, making impossible or painful for a packhorse to do the wrong thing will get it to act correctly.

Most horses that have been ridden will lead well. If a horse does not lead well, a little refresher course with a come-along or war bridle will solve the problem. The war bridle is not recommended for use by a novice. For more information on using a war bridle visit www.extension.org/pages/Young_Horse_Management_Series_Part_2.

DISPOSITION

Horses, LIKE PEOPLE, have a wide variety of dispositions. Some are kind and gentle and willing to do anything you ask. A few are mean and criminal. Enough good-natured horses exist to make it illogical and dangerous to keep a fractious horse that wants to kick, bite, and strike. If a horse has a completely negative attitude toward people and other horses, it should be replaced by one that accepts the work required by its owner.

Disposition in horses appears to be highly heritable. Some lines of horses have good dispositions and other families have bad ones. Unfortunately, too many horse breeders have tolerated poor dispositions while selecting horses for speed, action, and noble appearance. Disposition should carry more weight in the selection of breeding stock.

Good disposition is of greater importance now than 100 years ago. During that period, when everyone depended upon horses for transportation, the average person was a knowledgeable horse handler. Today, with the exception of ranch work, horses are primarily used for pleasure and recreation. Many riders do not ride very much and are ill equipped to handle a mean horse.

Horse Sense

A LARGE PART OF having horse sense is simply understanding what makes sense to a horse. A horse's two means of defense are kicking and running away. When threatened or surprised, a horse reacts immediately and instinctively by lashing out with its rear hooves or by bolting. If restrained from running, by being tied and packed with gear, it will panic and fight wildly to break that restraint. A twelve-hundred-pound animal in this mental state is a great danger, both to itself and its surroundings. Strange noises and objects, sudden movement, or unusual circumstances can spook a horse, and even a good-natured animal can be subject to panic. Remember this when you are around a horse, and you'll decrease your chances of getting hurt. A little care and forethought can prevent anyone from getting kicked, stepped on, or run over.

Once, when I was unsaddling a horse, one of my guests stepped out of a tent and started shaking the pine needles from his sleeping bag. A horse is not used to seeing something as big as a sleeping bag waving up and down in front of its face, and this horse, usually mild and good-natured, had a fit.

Throwing things can have the same effect. If members of your party want to play a little camp Frisbee, don't let them do it near the horses. Avoid tossing objects such as jackets, canteens, or sandwiches, to anyone near a horse. The spooked horse may have just been trying to duck, but the injured camper won't see it that way.

Move slowly around horses, and take particular care when other people are working around them. Walking up behind a horse unannounced is a good way to get kicked. When approaching, speak to the horse and let it know that you are there. Work at the horse's side rather than in front of or behind it.

When leading a horse, you'll have better control of the animal if you grasp the lead rope about twelve inches from the halter. Walk to one side rather than in front. Take care not to slip or stumble. The sudden movement of a fall could disconcert the horse. Never, repeat, never wrap the lead rope or reins around your hand or body. If the horse should bolt, you could be jerked or even dragged. When tying or untying your horse, keep your fingers out of any loop that could tighten if something frightened the horse.

A tethered horse in a panic is an explosion that doesn't stop until something gives, whether it's the halter, the rope, or the object it is tied to. Walking under a tied horse's neck invites such an explosion. It may sound contradictory, but you should always tie a horse to something that won't give. Otherwise, the frightened animal will gallop off, dragging the tent, dead tree, or grub box behind it.

Remember, a horse is a big, powerful animal, and can out-muscle even the strongest person.

Mules, Burros, and Llamas

MULES ARE WIDELY USED as pack stock throughout the United States and Canada. Burros are the traditional pack animal in the southwestern United States and in Mexico. The South American llama has also been introduced as pack stock in several places in the United States.

If a mule and a horse are getting the same amount of feed, the mule will usually do more work and stay in better shape. The mule will live longer than a horse, will be less likely to founder on either grain or water, and will be less likely to injure itself. Because of these advantages, many professional packers in the West use mules. The United States Army traditionally used mules for pack stock.

Mules are evidently more intelligent than horses and have a personality that makes working with them a little different than working with horses. If you are going to do something with a mule, you need to go ahead and do it with authority. If you hesitate or back off when a mule lays its ears back and lifts a hind leg, you aren't likely to get the job done. A mean mule can be very mean.

Lee Manes, who for years packed into the Selway-Bitterroot area of Idaho and the Wallowa Mountains of Oregon, once had a mule named Hitler that could kick you with one hind foot tied up. He also had a lot of good, honest mules and considered them superior to horses for use by professional packers.

In some areas, saddle mules have become popular for use on trail rides. Renewal of interest in

mules has stimulated shows like the Bishop, California, Mule Days, where mules compete in a wide variety of events including reining, driving, cutting, racing, and packing.

Since mules have a rather small foot in relation to their weight and tend to sink in soft ground and muskeg, they are not used to any extent in northern Canada and Alaska.

Burros were the pack animals of the old-time prospectors. They are used today by campers who hike and lead pack animals. A burro is not apt to overexert itself and will usually not walk as fast as a horse. If it gets tired, it will sometimes stop, lie down, and refuse to continue.

 Llamas are the pack animals of the Andes Mountains in South America. A llama can carry between 90 and 100 pounds. If it is overloaded, the llama will lie down. The llamas that are used in camping situations in California are led by a person on foot. Horses find that llamas take some getting used to.

Llamas eat grass and leaves, and require about one-third the amount of feed eaten by a horse. They do not have to be shod and are comfortable at high altitudes and in cold weather.

3. Tack

EQUIPMENT SUITED to horse camping adds to the camper's comfort and peace of mind. The difference between riding on a comfortable saddle and on one that is not is like the difference between feeling on top of the world and being at the bottom of a rockslide.

On one trail ride, I overheard a rider say, "To think that I paid good money to feel this miserable." Her problem was a very uncomfortable saddle. Some saddles are constructed in such a way that the rider feels like he is straddling a barrel. Others push the rider to the back of the saddle, leaving him with the awkward sensation of always being a step behind the movement of the horse. Use a saddle that is made for the comfort of the rider and horse, rather than one that is made for a five-second ride across the rodeo arena, or a few laps around a horse show ring.

Keep all your tack in good repair, and check it periodically for wear and tear. Neil Hatley, my father's cousin, learned that lesson the hard way. Neil was a packer, and he neglected to replace a frayed sling rope. The rope came apart out on the trail, dropping one pack. Because it was late in the day and the packhorse's cinch was no longer tight, the weight of the other pack caused the packsaddle to slide underneath the horse, and this caused the breeching to pull up under the horse's tail. When the dust finally settled from the ensuing fuss, there was little to salvage from either pack or packsaddle.

The gear in one's pack outfit can have a very humble beginning and then suddenly grow like Topsy. My pack outfit started in the late 1930s with one ancient sawbuck and two old riding saddles. My first purchase was a Decker packsaddle bought at a farm auction. It cost $12.50 and had the initials O.P.R. burned on the wooden bars. It turned out to be a saddle made by O.P. Robinette, the inventor of the Decker packsaddle.

I added more packsaddles as time went on by following classified ads in the newspaper, and by pursuing tips from friends. Eventually, the number of Deckers grew to twelve. I lost one on loan which was never returned, but a friend gave me another that brought the total back to twelve.

Riding saddles were added as more friends and relations wanted to go along on pack trips. The riding saddles were not very costly, as they were mostly high-backed saddles, which had gone out of style. Soon I had a dozen of them as well. By adding a saddle pad and new halters now and then, and a few manties each season, the outfit grew gradually in both quantity and quality. While my outfit has reached the size of those owned by some of the smaller professional outfitters, it has only been used for the pleasure of family and friends. A beginner can start horse camping with whatever equipment he already owns and by borrowing or improvising the rest. In time, the beginner will gain a sense of accomplishment from putting together a good, sound, usable pack outfit and keeping it in good repair.

HEAD GEAR

ORSES USED FOR EITHER riding or packing should be fitted with the strongest halter that money can buy. It should be made of nylon cord or web—nylon being the next thing to indestructible. Halters made of cotton cord eventually wear, and leather halters weaken with age. Sooner or later, a horse will jerk back, and if it is not tied with a stout halter, there will be a broken halter and a loose horse. The lead rope should be about ten feet long and made of strong 5/8-inch polypropylene rope with a sturdy cattle snap—the kind that will not come unsnapped.

For your saddle horse you will need a strong bridle with a throatlatch. A split ear bridle with no throatlatch can easily be rubbed off. Use a bit that the horse is accustomed to, and one-inch wide leather reins. Nylon reins or very narrow leather reins tend to slip through the hand. I happen to use rawhide reins and romal, but they are not the most practical for horse camping.

RIDING SADDLES

WHEN YOU START OUT horse camping, use any saddle you are accustomed to or find comfortable. It is socially acceptable to use an English or Australian saddle if that is what you have or like. Most riders will want to use saddlebags and tie a slicker or jacket to the saddle. Such attachments are made easier with a western saddle, but are not impossible with a non-western saddle. Simply cut your own saddle strings from rawhide, nylon cord, or baling twine, and attach the strings to the saddle's D-rings.

Rodeo cowboys had a strong influence on the western saddle design from the 1930s through the 1960s. During that time, the low back and low front needed by the rodeo roper and the bulldogger were incorporated into a large percentage of all saddles built. On many such saddles, the fork is so low that a horse with good withers will be galled. You should be able to slide your hand under the fork. A fork pressing on the saddle blanket is too low.

Saddles made for the ranch cowboy between 1890 and 1920 were made to be ridden all day. Such saddles had a higher fork and a higher back than the saddles developed for cowboys later on. Now, fortunately, the trend in western saddles has higher forks and backs.

Many saddles used for western show horses have conchos where the saddle strings would normally be located. If you have a choice, saddle strings are handy. A full double rigging often has the front cinch placed too far forward and will sometimes gall a horse near the elbow. A three-quarter rigging is well suited for horse camping. A center fire rigging will tend to move forward on the horse during a long, steep descent. If you have a center fire rigging, use a wide cinch. A back cinch is alright if you make sure that it stays attached to the front cinch, that it is tightened snugly, and that it is unhooked first when unsaddling. Otherwise, back cinches can cause a wreck. If you are not used to a back cinch and have trouble remembering what to

do with it, take it off and leave it in the saddle shed.

Saddlebags are handy and important pieces of equipment. They provide a place to carry lace leather, light rope or baler twine, a flashlight, lunch, and maybe a camera. Dr. Homer Webb, veterinarian on fifteen annual segments of the Chief Joseph Trail Ride, once commented, "There should be a law against big saddlebags. The bigger the bag, the more weight people stuff into them." Dr. Webb came to this conclusion after treating sore backs resulting from overloaded saddlebags. Pommel saddlebags, made one hundred years ago, and still available, put the extra weight on the front end of the horse where it was better able to carry it.

While a breast collar is useful if you are skidding poles or firewood, it is not necessary on most horses for keeping the saddle in place if the horse has good withers. A saddle is more likely to move forward going downhill than backward going uphill. A crupper or breeching will keep the saddle from slipping forward on a decline. In steep country and/or on hot days when a horse is sweaty, a breast collar might be useful to reduce the tendency of the saddle to slide backward.

A good saddle pad for horse camping should be thick to provide cushion, absorbent to soak up sweat, and washable. I prefer wool pads because they help maintain desired body heat, unlike some synthetic pads.

4. Packsaddles

SAWBUCK

PRIOR TO THE DEVELOPMENT of the Decker packsaddle, the sawbuck was used universally with pack animals. Since the sawbuck has now been replaced in many areas by the Decker, it is often possible to buy an inexpensive sawbuck. The sawbuck is usually double-rigged, and because it is made of wood, it is very light.

The beginning horse camper might want to use a sawbuck packsaddle because he can hang a pair of panniers on the sawbuck with a minimum of effort and skill, and be ready to go in a hurry. More experience is needed to put tents and sleeping bags on top of the panniers, to cover them with a manty, and to secure the pile to the saddle with a diamond hitch.

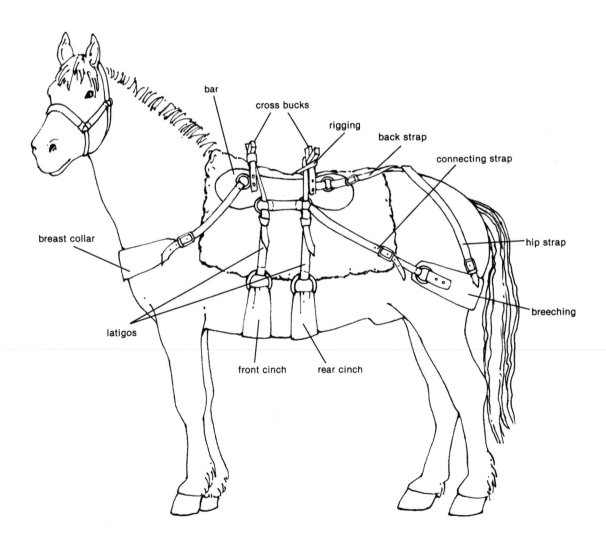

DECKER

THE DECKER PACKSADDLE was first developed by an Idaho packer named O.P. Robinette in the first part of the twentieth century. Robinette packed supplies into the mines during the Thunder Mountain gold rush using aparejo (pronounced ah-pah-ray-o) saddles, which originally came from Mexico and were widely used in California during the days of the forty-niners. Robinette was having trouble with his aparejos because they were galling the backs of his mules in hot weather.

Robinette believed that a better packsaddle and better system of packing could be developed. He used the same tree design as a Nez Perce man's saddle, which had forks made of deer horn covered with rawhide. Robinette kept the best feature of the aparejo, which was a large leather pad stuffed with grass, to give the pack animal some protection from the load.

The saddle became so popular that Robinette made over 12,000 trees, all with his O.P.R. initials burned onto the bars. This led people in Idaho to call the saddle an OPR rather than a Decker, the later manufacturer of the saddle originated by Robinette.

The Decker has broad, flat bars and is now made with iron or manganese-bronze arches or forks. A pad, called a half-breed boot, made with heavy canvas stuffed with deer hair, horsehair, or dry bear grass, covers the saddle. The pad protects the horse and makes it possible to pack unusual cargo without danger. The Decker it usually rigged center fire and uses a wide cinch with tie-down rings near the cinch ring. It can be packed easily by an experienced hand.

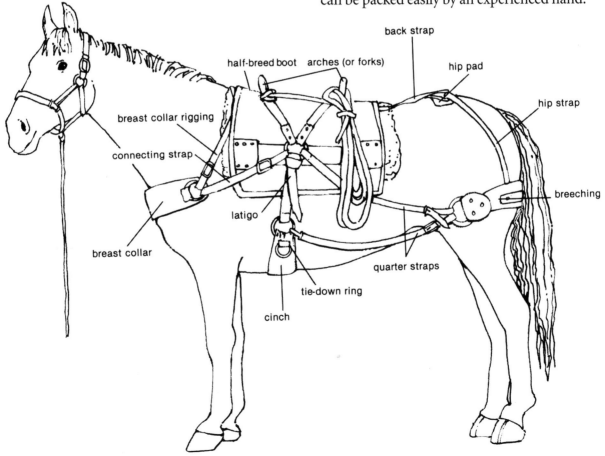

FITTINGS

THE MOST IMPORTANT accessory for the packsaddle is a thick saddle pad. It should be about twice as thick as that used under a riding saddle. A rider can help his horse along by riding correctly, but a pack is dead weight and requires more padding. The extra thick, quilted pad is the one to use.

With the sawbuck you will need a 45-foot, 5/8-inch manila lash rope braided into the ring of a lash cinch. Add a 6' x 8' canvas manty or pack cover and a pair of panniers, which are described later.

For a Decker you'll want to have two 30-foot, 1/2-inch sling ropes braided into the front fork. Each Decker will need two 7' x 8' manties made of 18-ounce canvas, and two 30-foot, 3/8-inch manty ropes. A manty could be compared to a sheet of wrapping paper and the cargo ropes to the string that ties the wrapping around the package. The manty holds the pack together and protects it from rain or dust.

Both sawbuck and Decker saddles need pigtails. A pigtail is a 4-foot long, 1/4- or 3/8-inch rope with each end braided into the saddle ring and the remainder run under the rear fork (or buck). This pigtail is an equine trailer safety hitch for hooking on the next packhorse. The lead rope of the second packhorse will be tied into the pigtail of the first.

Panniers

THE CONTAINERS that hang on each side of a sawbuck are known as panniers, alforjas, or kyacks in different parts of the continent. Traditionally these containers were made of canvas with leather ends; some were made of wood, wicker, metal, and more recently, of plastic or fiberglass. Canvas panniers are best for packing soft cargo, rigid ones for anything that could break or mash. All will have ropes or traps that go around the bucks on the sawbuck. Straps with buckles can be hooked to the forks of a Decker.

HORSESHOES

Most horse camping takes place in mountainous and rocky areas, and rocks wear horses' feet off faster than they can grow. Horseshoes prevent breaking or wearing on the wall of the hoof. While shoes provide protection, they might also cause the hoof to become too dry. When a horse is not being used enough to wear the hoof down, it should be left barefooted. This is true in places like Florida, where the soft, sandy soil doesn't wear on hooves.

Flat plates are satisfactory for most horse trips. If the trails are unusually steep, or if flat plates become slick when wet, a calked shoe is helpful but should be avoided unless absolutely necessary. Calked shoes are more harmful than flat plates if a horse kicks another horse or a person, and they churn up trails, causing dust and then erosion during heavy rains.

Shoes should be reset every four to six weeks. Otherwise the horse's hooves become too long and grow over the shoes, or become contracted.

To pick up a front foot, stand beside the horse facing toward its rump, run your hand down the leg to the lower part of the cannon bone near the fetlock and pinch the area between the bone and tendons. The horse should pick its foot up. If this doesn't work, gently nudge the horse away from you to get some weight off the foot, then pull the foot up by the fetlock. To lift the hind foot, stand next to the horse facing rearward, run your hand down the leg, and pull up and forward on the lower cannon. Once the leg is brought up, it can be moved back to be worked on.

When shoeing, trim and then rasp the foot flat. Shape the shoe until it fits the foot. Direct the nails outward rather than inward toward the live, sensitive part of the foot, and have them centered on the foot's white line. Twist off the protruding nail immediately after it is driven. When all nails have been driven, clinch them tightly by holding a camp ax head or rasp against the severed nail and giving each nail several brisk raps with the hammer. Rasping off any hoof that protrudes past the shoe will complete the job.

A horse with sore feet is a lame horse. If no one in the party can shoe a horse, pack a couple of Easyboots in case a horse loses a shoe. They just slip over the hoof—if you can put on your own socks in the morning, you can put on an Easyboot.

Repair Kit

U SE GEAR THAT IS strong and durable, and maintain it well—then you won't have broken equipment when you are days away from the saddle shop. The best way to reduce the need for emergency repair is to examine the equipment carefully well in advance of going on a trip.

Check the condition of the latigos and cinches on the saddles and replace any missing saddle strings. After checking every strap on the harness of the packsaddles, replace any that have become cracked or broken. Check the sling ropes, lash ropes, and pigtails for broken or frayed strands. Go over panniers for rips and holes and test the traps that hold them onto the saddle.

Upon returning from a trip, clean all the leather equipment and rub in neat'sfoot oil, using the pure oil and not the compound variety. Then, if repaired and properly stored, the tack will require little or no maintenance before the next trip.

Equipment should be stored where there is some moisture, but not enough to cause mold. A basement is fine if it is not too damp. On the other hand, leather loses its life if it becomes too dry, which often happens in attics and upstairs storerooms.

If a barn, storage shed, or saddle shed is used, check to see that it is kept free of rats and mice. They will eat straps for the salt and make nests of saddle pads.

On the trail, an equipment repair kit should be carried in a saddlebag where it will be handy. Included in the kit should be lace leather and a knife with a leather punch. A little zip-tie, a pair of pliers or fence tool, duct tape, and some baler twine would be helpful at times.

5. Gear

Life's necessities are food, clothing, and shelter. Making certain the horse camper is provided these necessities in a primitive environment far removed from any source of supply is one of the purposes of this book. If a horse camper packs back into the wilderness for a week and neglects to bring something important along, there is no convenient way to resupply. People who have never been cold, wet, and hungry do not thoroughly appreciate being warm, dry, and well-fed.

The biggest and probably the warmest and most comfortable bed that I have ever packed belonged to Ed Janeway. It was one of the first king-size, extra-thick sleeping bags with fitted snaps encasing it in a bed tarp—custom-made to Ed's specifications. Ed had cowboyed in the days when cowboys slept on the ground and ate from the chuck wagon. He knew what it took for him to be comfortable on a pack trip. I used to kid him that it took one horse just to carry his bed. But Ed was the kind of guest whose company was well worth an extra horse. An excellent horseman, he was always willing to ride the colt that was on its first pack trip or to lead the first-time packhorse.

Since the days of Ed's big camp bed, equipment companies have made great strides toward improving design and materials used in tents, sleeping bags, and camp stoves. But the beginner doesn't have to start out with large expenditures for new equipment. Often gear that you don't have can be borrowed from family or friends. The present tendency is to go light, thus requiring fewer horses and reducing impact on the environment.

The first pack trip for which I helped assemble equipment was in the autumn of 1938. I was going to miss a week of school and accompany my dad on an elk hunt. The economic ills of the Depression were still with us. There were no trips to the sporting goods or dry goods stores. Even the grocery benefited little from our trip. We had an ancient wall tent that had been in the family much longer than I. Bedrolls were put together with the blankets and quilts we used at home. At the time, our mattresses were made of fir boughs cut when we reached camp, a practice now discouraged because of overuse. Our first-aid kit consisted of a bottle of Mercurochrome, a couple pieces of bed sheet, adhesive tape, a jar of Mentholatum and some dried chicken gizzard lining, a home remedy for digestive complaints.

The cooking outfit was fresh from mother's kitchen, and it included pots and pans that she considered expendable. Warped and dented, most had suffered accidents of some kind. The camp stove was a homemade wood burner. The stovepipe was put inside the stove when packed. Our clothing was what we normally worked or rode in.

We packed eight miles up the Selway River, had a great week of hunting, and came home with a winter's supply of meat. Later, we would go on summer pack trips for recreation, fishing, and sightseeing. The camp outfit was gradually improved. Upgrading it over forty-three years was next best to using it.

TENTS

CANVAS WALL TENTS have long been the standby of outfitters and old-time horse campers. They require poles that must be set up correctly and are fairly heavy. Newer tent designs, such as the teepee, dome, and pup tents, have an aluminum or fiberglass framework that can be collapsed and packed with the tent. Having their own framework, such tents require less time and effort in setting up. This is important in areas where wooden tent poles cannot be made on the spot.

Wall tents are well suited to the professional outfitter because they are roomy, can accommodate a stove for late fall hunting trips, and are usually used at campsites where tent poles can be made. Tent poles should be leaned up against a tree when not in use to prevent them from rotting. Don't use them for firewood.

Choose a tent with a floor. It not only keeps you and your gear cleaner and drier, it also excludes unwelcome crawling guests. Look for material that is water repellent, lightweight, fire retardant, and strong. Waterproof materials which do not breathe can cause condensation on the inside, making it wetter inside the tent than outside. Material is now available that is both waterproof and breathable. Otherwise, you will need a waterproof fly over a breathable tent to keep yourself dry. Flies take time to put up and have a tendency to blow away in high winds.

Try to find a tent that is easy to put up. I once watched a couple spend three hours trying to set up a complicated small dome tent. They painstakingly read pages of directions and finally concluded they needed the help of a factory representative. Set up a new tent in your backyard to avoid getting caught as they did. I prefer to reduce the visual impact of the camp by using tents of dull shades of green or brown rather than the bright colors now available. Weight is not as important here as with backpacking.

SLEEPING

SLEEPING COMFORTABLY and warmly on a camping trip is almost as vital to a good disposition as being well fed. Before buying a new sleeping bag, figure out the temperature range you expect and then buy a bag that is more than adequate. At high altitudes in the middle of summer, there will be frosty nights and ice in the water pail—no matter where you are.

For many years, down-filled sleeping bags were the best. Now there are synthetic insulation materials that approach down in warmth. Although more bulky, a fiber-filled bag will continue to keep you warm even if it is wet, while a down bag won't.

If your sleeping bag does not keep you warm, use a wool blanket on the inside. If you find that you do not have enough bedding once you have packed in, lay your clothes and coats over the top of the sleeping bag, cover them with a manty, and tuck its edges under the bag. The manty will keep the clothes from falling off the bag and will add some insulation. They will be heavy, but heavy is better than cold.

Air mattresses or foam pads will provide cushioning under bag. The air mattress is an exhausting device to inflate and most of them will let you down eventually. If you own one and it is still working, use it. Otherwise, get a foam pad. A three-inch foam pad is bulky but light. If necessary, pads can be top-packed in order not to take up space.

Even if you are over-age and have a touch of "rumatiz," with a warm bag and a thick foam pad, you can sleep like a baby.

First Aid

A FIRST-AID KIT is like fire insurance—you hardly ever need it, but when you do, it is a necessity. Its contents should be chosen specifically for horse camping trips, bearing in mind the area you are packing into. There is no point in taking snakebite kit if there area no poisonous snakes.

Galen Rogers was the medical doctor on the Chief Joseph Trail ride for thirteen years. During the accumulated 13,000 horse camping days for which he was responsible, there were only three accidents which prevented a rider from finishing the ride. All three riders were unhorsed: one while mounting, one when the horse came over backwards, and one while crossing a creek. Most of Dr. Rogers' work involved treating sunburn and dispensing Furacin salve for sore fannies. Once when there were 380 riders on the trail, he had to send to town for more suppositories for the relief of hemorrhoids. He recommends the following:

- Cortisone cream (burns, sunburn, and abrasions)
- Furacin salve (saddle sores and blisters)
- Kaopectate (diarrhea)
- Dialose Plus (constipation)
- Pepto-Bismol (stomach-ache)
- Merthiolate (cuts)
- Anelgesic tablets (pain)
- Antihistamines (colds, allergies)
- Bee-sting kit
- Dressings, tape, and bandages
- Elastic bandage (sprains)
- Fep cream (bites)
- Rubbing alcohol
- Sling and tourniquet
- Needle and thread
- Safety pins
- Iodine (water purification)
- Tweezers
- Murine (eyes)
- Universal antidote (poisoning)
- Red Cross First-Aid Manual

BASIC HORSE CARE

ALWAYS TAKE ALONG a brush and curry comb to keep your horse clean. This helps prevent sores and galls, particularly on the horse's back and sides. I take along a bell for the bell mare when the horses are grazing. It helps keep the horses together, lets you know where they are, and is musical. If there are other campers in the area who might not enjoy the bell, don't use it. Each to his own—the roar of a motorcycle is musical to some people.

If any of the horses are broke to stake, take along a stake rope. Hobbles won't prevent a horse from leaving, but they will slow it down. Being hobbled often encourages a horse to stay put and graze where it is rather than roaming all over the country. Chain hobbles are very strong but are also heavy and bulky, while double ring hobbles are lighter, but not as durable. Rawhide hobbles need moisture and beef fat to remain smooth and pliable. If they are allowed to become dry and hard, they'll skin up a horse's ankles. Rawhide hobbles should not be used for a grazing horse, but only for a short period of time in lieu of tying the horse up.

The most useful horse medicine to take along is furacin salve for galls and wounds. Stretch gauze and cotton are useful for leg injuries. The medicine kit should also include a bottle of penicillin, several 12-milliliter disposable syringes with 18-gauge needles, a small plastic bottle of scarlet oil, and a dozen phenybutazone (bute) pills, or tube of the medication in paste form. Bute is an anti-inflammatory, somewhat similar to aspirin, and will help sooth mild lamenesses, a sore back, and other equine ills.

Horses don't need much medical care on pack trips, but having some medicine along makes people feel more comfortable. Horses managed to survive centuries before the first veterinarian was given a license to practice. Most horse health problems are caused by people doing something wrong with the horse, not by the horse doing anything to itself.

FIREARMS

FIREARMS ARE RARELY used, but taking one along can make the camping party feel more comfortable. Make certain that there is someone who is knowledgeable about gun safety and who is competent to use a gun. Firearms should be handled as though there were bullets coming out of the barrel at all times. Having a firearm along that no one knows how to use is more dangerous than having no firearm at all.

The Pikes Peak Riders had a strict no firearms rule. One year a horse got itself tangled up in some logs, breaking its leg. It had to be destroyed. There was no firearm. To club or stone a horse to death has to be painful for the horse and traumatic for the people. The next year, the trail boss carried a firearm. It is extremely rare that a horse has to be destroyed, but if that rare occurrence happens, a firearm is a godsend.

A cautionary note about destroying animals—horses do have recuperative powers, and if they have an accident or take a few rolls down a hill, they should not arbitrarily be "put out of their misery." Before applying euthanasia, be sure that recovery is impossible.

One autumn I was installing stays in a fence out in summer range country. I had packed the stays in on horses and was busy installing them when an elk hunter shot near my horse. The second shot went through the horse's gaskin, halfway between the hock and stifle. The bone was not broken, but the horse was bleeding profusely. Full of regret, the hunter offered to put my horse out of its misery. "Hold on there," I said, "The bone isn't broken and if you'll lead the horse, I'll hold the wound shut with my hand so the horse won't bleed to death before we can get out of here." And so we led the horse out, my hand covering the bullet hole. A neighbor took me to my truck, and I hauled the horse to the vet. The horse was completely healed in a month.

Recognize that your horse camping party will likely be out of touch with the outside world. If your group is attacked, you cannot necessarily pick up a telephone and call the sheriff's office. While I have no personal knowledge of such attacks actually happening, I have heard of isolated incidents. If you are concerned about this, packing a firearm might make the party feel easier and might discourage possible troublemakers.

Wild animal problems are as remote a danger as wild people problems. The occasional moose will refuse to give ground, and a shot into the ground will frighten it away (and will also shake up the horses). Once in a while, a lazy bear will find it easier to rob camps than to make an honest living.

Do not shoot any game animal unless the season is open and you have a valid hunting license and tag, or unless someone's life is threatened, or you are facing starvation. Check local regulations about gun permits in the area of your trip. My horse packing guests feel comfortable with firearms, and I carry a .357 magnum or .38 Special.

COOKING

A BASIC GROUP COOKING KIT for six people should be sufficient, as pack trip parties are rarely larger than that. Stainless steel weighs more than aluminum, but is much more durable and easier to clean. A compact kit with three kettles and two frying pans will do nicely. The square lid from an old Maytag washing machine makes a handy camp grill. My two aluminum dishpans—one for washing and one for rinsing—fit together.

A large, old-style gallon coffee pot doesn't waste space because so much stuff can be packed inside it. If you have a small sheepherder's stove with an oven for biscuits, you'll need a pan that will fit in the

oven. If you don't have a stove, take along a Dutch oven. Your decision to include the Dutch oven should balance its weight against your love for biscuits, cobbler, and hot bread.

I take along two extra plates, cups, bowls, and place settings than there are people on the trip. My preference is for Melmac plates, which are strong and pleasant to eat from, and stainless steel flatware. Cooking utensils include two each of long serving spoons, spatulas, and cooking forks, and one ladle and a can opener. For cleaning up, bring several two-gallon canvas water buckets, biodegradable soap, scouring pads, potholders, dishrags, and dish towels. Plastic bags can be used to take out unburnable trash, and don't forget the matches.

I prefer cooking on metal rather than over an open fire—cooking is more even, my hands don't get burned, and the pans aren't covered with soot. I carry a 24-inch x 17-inch, 16-gauge metal sheet fastened by wood screws to the back of one of my grub boxes of the same size. It only weighs four pounds and makes cooking much easier than over an open fire. A slightly more civilized stove would be one of the lightweight wood burners that are available.

If you are packing into an area without firewood, take a gas or propane stove. A propane stove and fuel weigh more than a gas stove and its fuel, but a propane stove is almost foolproof. There is no danger of gas spilling on anything or of having a blowup. The fuel is also more expensive, but the lack of trouble is worth the added cost. A two-burner stove is adequate for a small party of campers.

CLOTHING

BOOTS

The type of footwear worn for horse camping will depend upon where you are going and what you will be doing when you get there. If the side trips from camp will be spent entirely on horseback, cowboy boots are good to wear. However, the slick leather soles on cowboy boots can cause slipping and sliding on the ground. The horse camper will stay on his feet better with rubber or composition soles. The packer needs all the traction he can get when lifting the heavy packs onto the horses. If campers intend to do any extensive walking or climbing, they need to wear laced-up walking shoes that give good traction on rocks and support the ankles.

Lew Portnoy wore leather-soled cowboy boots on the pack trip arranged to take photographs for this book. To get the photographs he wanted, Lew occasionally needed to get off his horse and climb around on steep and rocky hillsides. He quickly determined that it would have been better to be riding in hiking boots rather than hiking in riding boots.

On the other hand, don't wear hiking shoes with wide, thick soles, which could hang up in the stirrups. Footwear should also protect you in case a horse steps on your foot. Horses sometimes step to one side to keep their balance. They are not maliciously trying to stomp on the rider's foot, although it might seem that way. Do not wear oxfords, tennis shoes, boating shoes, or any type of canvas shoe.

Lace-up boots can be laced loosely when riding. This frees the ankle joint in order to keep the heel down. The lacing can be tightened up for walking. There is a boot called "the packer" which has cowboy boot heels, but is laced for ankle support and has good traction. There is also a "patrol" boot used by motorcycle policemen. This type of boot has elastic lacing at the ankles that stretches for riding, but gives sufficient support for walking.

RIDING CLOTHES

RIDING CLOTHES NEED TO BE comfortable and functional. The most fashionable rider on a pack trip is the one whose garments give the most protection from the elements and from contact with the saddle. Leave the urban cowboy clothes at home.

Most horse campers wear western jeans such as Levis, Wranglers, or Lees. So-called "designer jeans" are not manufactured for riding and are not good horse camping clothes. Some riders prefer English breeches or jodhpurs, as these garments have a chamois-lined crotch and seamless, set-in knee patches. The riding pants you choose should be comfortable and broken in. Don't wear them new.

You can minimize chafing and galling by wearing long underwear or tights under your pants. Some endurance riders, including men, wear panty hose for that purpose.

Any comfortable shirt with a tail long enough to stay put will work well as a riding shirt. Long sleeves, which can be rolled up in hot weather and rolled down in cool weather or as protection from the sun, are a better choice than short sleeves. A felt western hat protects the head from the rain and sun. A western straw hat is comfortable in very hot weather. Watch out that you don't lose it to a tree branch or gust of wind. Actually, any hat with a brim will protect your head, so there's no need to feel out of place if you don't have a western hat.

Veteran trail rider Juli Thorson recommends a bra with support for any woman planning to ride several hours a day. Thorson, who has often ridden fifty miles a day on endurance rides, says many women will be most comfortable wearing cotton or cotton-lined underwear.

A cotton bandana is one of the most useful and versatile articles you can wear on a horse camping trip. Roll it on the diagonal and knot it around your neck. On cool mornings, it will keep you warmer by keeping wind off your neck. On hot afternoons, dip the bandana in cool water and tie it back on. You will feel much cooler. A bandana can also be used as a handkerchief, bandage, washcloth, or tourniquet.

Gloves are a necessity for preventing scratches, scrapes, and sunburn. The most comfortable ones for riding and packing are made of buckskin.

COLD AND HOT

RIDING A HORSE IN COLD WEATHER without proper clothes can be a bone-chilling experience. Hunting trips in the fall commonly involve cold weather riding.

Wear insulated, long underwear. Socks should be thick and made of wool. Footwear needs to be insulated and waterproof. Malone and Woolrich both make good, heavy wool pants. A down-filled vest over a wool shirt adds warmth without binding the arms. Hip-length jackets, whether down or wool, are warmer than waist-length jackets.

Chaps add a little warmth. A saddle slicker that is a size too big and fits over your thick clothes will keep you dry if it snows and warm if it is windy. Warm headgear is a must. A fur hat with earflaps is the best, but wool hats also work well. If the outside cover of the hat is not waterproof, bring a plastic cover that is. Cold weather riding gear needs to give the rider enough freedom of movement to mount a horse, yet keep him warm once mounted.

Mittens are the best cold weather covering for hands. Although clumsy and awkward, they are warm. A heavy wool mitten worn inside a waterproof nylon over-mitten will do the best job of keeping hands both warm and dry.

In hot, desert regions, a billed cap with a large kerchief hanging out Foreign Legion-style is excellent protection from the sun and won't get blown or knocked off. In desert mountains, it might be 25° F. on waking in the high country, and 100° on the valley floor at 3 p.m. If you dress in numerous layers of light clothing, you can cool off by shedding them one by one.

RAIN

A SADDLE SLICKER IS THE BEST KIND of rain gear for riding because it extends over the legs and keeps the rain and snow off the saddle. The old-time slicker often cracked and tore, but the modern ones are made of new materials that are both waterproof and very tough. While ponchos give good protection from the rain, they are a problem in the wind. Their fluttering and popping can spook the horses.

Most western wear stores stock plastic hat covers that make a rain hat of all western hats, felt or straw. Overshoes and overboots are available. For midsummer trips, the thin, light-weight types are adequate. For late fall, however, the heavy, lined, high-topped kinds are best.

Rubber overboots are not only good to have in the rain, they are also handy to wear first thing in the morning, when there is dew on the grass.

CHAPS

CHAPS (or "leggings" as they are called in the Southwest United States) are a good piece of gear to have, but they are not necessary. They protect the legs from trees, rocks, brush, and weather, and from being torn up if the rider makes an unscheduled landing.

Chaps come in two general styles called "batwings" and "shotguns." The batwings fold around the legs and are hooked together with three snaps. They are quick to put on or take off, but can be drafty when riding downwind.

The name "shotguns" is used for a style of chaps which, when closed, look like the barrel of a double-barreled shotgun. They resemble a pair of pants legs that are tied together at the top and are supported by a belt. Contemporary shotguns have a big, heavy zipper, which closes them around the legs. Before zippers, getting into shotguns took some doing. The traditional angora chaps were shotguns and gave a lot of warm protection. Shotguns are a little warmer than batwings, but if the zipper fails, you end up with batwings without snaps. Most shotguns are made of lightweight, more flexible leather than batwings. They are a bit more comfortable and a little warmer than batwings, but provide less protection. I use batwings and keep three extra pairs for guests who want to use them.

6. Food

Eating is one of the basic pleasures of life. The added exercise and enthusiasm that accompany seeing new places and doing new things on a pack trip stimulate the appetite. Aromas and flavors come through clearly in the wilderness. Food tastes better than usual.

You'll be lucky to have someone in your party who enjoys cooking. A good camp cook has been a treasured species throughout history. Almost anyone can cook a can of beans or fry bacon, but someone who knows how to make cornbread in a Dutch oven, or brings along a few spices for the stew, is a real friend.

Doctor Welty, a guest who lived near the Mexican border, preferred cooking gourmet meals for our hunting party to searching for elk. It was an enjoyable division of labor on both sides. Instead of having just eggs for breakfast, we would be served huevos rancheros; instead of a dinner of liver and onions, we would get barbecued ribs in a wonderful sauce.

I try to do the grocery shopping with other members of the party so that everyone gets what he wants. Often the campers will live in the same area and can get together to plan the food. Then, the group can take off the grocery list any items that no one particularly wants. Having a small family orchard, I always take a good supply of dried peaches, apricots, apple, and prunes. Once, without inquiring whether or not my guests liked prunes, I cooked up a kettle full. When I tried to serve them, everyone graciously said no thanks, and I ended up eating a lot of prunes.

MENUS

HERE ARE TWO WAYS of organizing the food for a pack trip. One way is to make out a menu for each meal taking only the ingredients necessary to prepare the foods on the menu. The other approach is to take along enough of the right type of food for all the meals to be eaten, but to make specific decisions about combination of dishes as you travel.

With an organized menu, you can plan ahead when packing the grub boxes by arranging the meals in the order in which you need them. Such planning also lessens the chance of having to pack out any leftovers when the trip is ended.

My friend, Ester Hibbs, carefully plans the food for the horse trips that she and her husband Earl take. They ranched for years in Hells Canyon where packing was a necessity—the ranch head-quarters were thirty miles from the nearest road. Ester is a mas-ter with the camp menu. By the time the horses are unpacked, unsaddled, and the tents put up, she has the evening meal ready to eat.

Ester plans the trip itinerary by the number of miles and riding hours in a day to know how much time she will have to prepare the meals. Early in the trip, she might fix a breakfast of dehydrated juice, bacon and eggs, and hotcakes

with butter and syrup. Lunch on the trail will be lunchmeat or ham sandwiches, an orange or apple, and candy or granola bar. Dinner might be steak, hash browns, vegetable, salad, and canned fruit or a cake from home. At the early stage in the trip, she can still use fresh meat.

Later in the trip, you will have to rely on canned and dried foods. Breakfast, then, would be oatmeal and raisins or dates, and canned ham, canned hash browns, or French toast made with stale bread and dehydrated eggs. For lunch there would be peanut butter sandwiches, canned fruit or pudding, and a candy bar or cookies. Dinner would include a western stew of canned meat, potatoes, carrots, and onions. Dried or canned fruit could be served directly from the can, or cooked into a cobbler.

Once Ester has figured out the menu for each specific meal on the trip, she then totals the different foods up for the final grocery list. On my trips, I take the less specific approach mentioned earlier. I always try to make certain that I have enough of each kind of food for each meal, but I never make out a menu that specifies when each dish will be served. Other than serving the more perishable foods first, I enjoy the flexibility of cooking whatever the majority of the group happens to be in the mood for that particular day. Some foods might be more appealing after an especially strenuous day, and others after a day of rest.

Whether for health reasons or by custom, people often prefer specific foods. Someone going into the wilderness for a week should not be subjected to a drastic change in diet. I once packed photographer Marshall Faber into the Big Horn Crags. Marshall had diabetes, and we built the menu around his requirements. We all ate well, and he stayed healthy.

RECIPES

JERKY

2 lbs. flank or round steak
Marinade
¼ c. soy sauce
1 t. Worcestershire sauce
½ t. liquid smoke
¼ t. coarse ground pepper
¼ t. garlic powder
½ t. onion powder
1 t. salt

Trim the fat from the meat and cut it in ¼-inch strips. Mix the marinade in a blender. Pour the mixture over the meat strips in a bowl, cover, and let set in the refrigerator for one day, shaking and turning the bowl every few hours. Preheat oven to 175° F. Shake excess sauce from the meat and lay the strips out on a wire rack in a flat pan. Bake 5 to 6 hours. Cool and store in jars in the refrigerator.

WESTERN STEW

2 lbs. canned beef in stock or gravy
4 T. oil or margarine
4 carrots
2 onions
2 turnips
1 sm. cabbage
6 potatoes
salt and pepper
thyme, sage, or packaged seasoning

Since the meat is already cooked, the vegetables need only be browned in the margarine or oil, covered with water, simmered until tender, combined with the heated meat, and seasoned to taste. Brown the onions, turnips, carrots, and cabbage in that order and cook the potatoes last, either in the stew broth or separately. Season and thicken, if necessary. If potatoes are cooked separately, the rest of the stew can be served over them.

BANNOCK BREAD

A backcountry bread that is easy to make

2 1/3 c. Bisquick
2/3 c. water
oil or margarine

Mix the Bisquick with the water and knead
until the mass forms a smooth ball. Make patties four to six inches wide and ½-inch thick.
Punch a hole in the center. Fry the patties in the
heated oil or margarine until the bottoms are
browned, about 10 minutes over an open fire.
Tip the pan to a 75° angle to the coals so that the
top of the bread will brown. Serve with butter
or margarine, and jam or honey.

FRUIT DUMPLINGS

4 c. fresh, dried, or canned fruit
2 c. Bisquick
2/3 c. water
canned or dried cream or milk (reconstituted)

Reconstitute dried fruit by soaking in water
overnight or by boiling in enough water to
cover. Simmer fresh fruit in enough water to
cover, or bring canned fruit to a boil in its syrup.
Prepare the dumplings by mixing the Bisquick
and water. Drop spoonfuls of dumpling mixture into the boiling fruit, cover, and simmer for
fifteen minutes. Serve for dessert with reconstituted cream or milk.

UPSIDE-DOWN COBBLER

¼ lb. margarine
2/3 c. sugar
2/3 c. water
1 c. Bisquick
1 t. vanilla
4 c. native fruit

Cream the margarine and sugar. Add Bisquick,
vanilla, and water. Mix well and pour into a
greased Dutch oven. Spread huckleberries, ser-
viceberries, thimbleberries, elderberries, black-
berries, or whatever native fruit is in season on
top of the dough. Bake until brown. Dough will
rise to the top, and fruit will sink to the bottom.

Nutrition

The nineteenth century mountain man lived off the country. He was a horse camper who had a high protein, high-energy diet composed largely of meat. Unfortunately, he did not know anything about nutrition and often suffered from a lack of vitamin C. There were several native sources of vitamin C that he could have used, but he didn't know what they were, or even that he needed them.

The modern horse camper can get his vitamin C from citrus fruits, tomatoes, potatoes, and other fresh fruits and vegetables. He can get vitamin A from cheese, butter, milk, and eggs. Cheese keeps well under horse camping conditions. Milk can be reconstituted and margarine can be used instead of butter. Fresh eggs last surprisingly long, especially at higher altitudes.

Unlike the mountain man living off wild game or the cowboy living off an occasional beef from his herd, today's horse packer will get his protein from freshly caught fish, cured, dried, or canned meat, or canned fish or poultry. Fresh or frozen meat can be taken along and eaten during the first several days. Do not try to use fresh meat after too long in warm weather. Vegetarians have it easier with beans, lentils, nuts, and cereal products.

The old-time camp cook with his chuck wagon probably fed the cowboys a bit too much of biscuits, bacon, and beans instead of vegetables and fruits. In addition to vitamins, vegetables supply some of the bulk that keeps the digestive system working. Plan a larger breakfast if the day's activities include heavier work such as clearing trails, climbing mountains, or hiking into a high mountain lake.

BREAKFAST

A NUTRITIOUS AND TASTY breakfast gets the horse camper off to a good start. Bacon, eggs, and pancakes with fruit juice and coffee and/or hot chocolate make a breakfast that most campers are willing to get up for. Vary the menu by frying, scrambling, or boiling the eggs. If huckleberries (or blueberries) are in season, throw a half-cup in with the pancake batter. Alternate hash browns with pancakes, and ham with bacon. Plan for sausage the first morning because sausage doesn't keep as well as other meat.

Eggs are one of the most nutritious foods that can be taken on a pack trip. They are worth the little extra care needed to pack them. Butter is awkward on pack trips because it melts in hot weather and is hard to spread when it's cold. Margarine is less sensitive to temperature. The kind that comes in a plastic squeeze bottle removes all risk. Plastic bottles are also handy for syrup and other liquids because they don't break or rattle. Powdered milk or dry coffee creamer is lighter in weight and easier to handle than canned milk.

If cooking is done with wood, cut enough firewood the evening before for the breakfast fire. If kindling and firewood are ready to go, the first person up can start the fire and get the coffee pot on. Some people cannot tolerate a long interval between the time they arise and that first cup of coffee.

Ham, eggs, sliced bacon, sliced bread, and sliced lunchmeat will usually last for a week's trip in cold weather. If it is warmer, take storage and food safety issues into consideration. If the weather is hot, fresh meat will be good for only the first day, and the trip will have to be finished on canned and dried foods.

LUNCH

THE PRIMARY LUNCH menu is based on sandwiches. Lunch is often eaten on a side trip from the main camp along a new trail en route to a new vista or an off-trail lake.

Vary the sandwiches from day to day. Use any meat left over from breakfast first. There is a tremendous variety of lunchmeats. Chicken and turkey are good substitutes for the more common ham or beef. As the meat is used up, or if the weather is hot, sandwiches can be made from canned tuna or peanut butter in one of its infinite combinations. Add an orange or apple, and finish off with a cookie or two. Carrots keep a long time, are rich in vitamin A, and provide some moisture when the sandwiches are too dry. I take some dried fruit or jerky for between meal snacks.

Take plastic bags and paper sacks along for packing your lunch. The plastic bags will keep the food fresh, and the paper sack will keep it from getting mixed up with everything else in your saddlebag. If you are eating at camp, a bowl of soup is a nice addition to a sandwich lunch.

Supper

Planning a simple main dish for the first evening in camp makes it easy on the cook and means that everyone will be fed in a hurry. Prior to a pack trip, I will make a batch of beef stew and a pot of beans or lentils. I can keep these dishes frozen until the pack trip, when they will make a quick and easy first-night's supper along with some tossed salad, canned peaches, and cookies. Lettuce doesn't keep for long and has to be used early on the trip.

If you heat water, people can choose between coffee, tea, and hot chocolate. Cold water can be used to mix milk or powdered fruit drinks. If you are taking frozen meat, have it frozen in the size portions you need in camp. Take along canned poultry and ham and alternate with beef stew and steak for the main evening dish. It's easy to have a different vegetable every supper, and while I am content to eat potatoes all the time, others might prefer whole corn or a pot of rice. I take green tomatoes along and eat them as they ripen on the trip. Once they are gone, you'll still have raw carrots.

Canned fruit can be alternated with dried fruit, which is easier to pack and weighs very little. People with a sweet tooth should be allowed free access to cookies, which are lightweight and keep well. Packaged pudding mixes are easy to prepare on the trail. When checking out the menu with the party before you leave, find out whether people want white or dark bread.

DRINK

OST "MAKINS" for things to drink weigh very little, and it is easy to bring along everyone's favorite drink. A dozen extra tea bags for the tea drinker in the group are no trouble. Fresh milk is very short-lived, but there are now some brands of dried milk on the market that taste much better than earlier types. Canned fruit juices are heavy because they contain so much water. They taste better than the dry mixes, but I leave them out and save on weight.

In most horse camping situations, the water is unusually good. After drinking mountain water for a week, town water is hard to take. However, with the increasing use of public lands comes an increasing possibility of contaminated water. For many years, I carried only a collapsible cup, getting my drinks along the trail when I was thirsty. Unfortunately, contamination is now so widespread that all natural sources of water on the trail should be considered unsafe to drink and be treated with iodine, boiled, or put through another water purification process before use.

Horse Feed

MANY OF THE COMMON AREAS for horse camping are well grassed and provide adequate horse feed. Since horses eat grass, and most big game animals feed on low bushes or small trees, there is no competition for food. The impact of horse grazing depends upon the amount of use and the season. Close grazing should be avoided when the grass is young.

Early in the season, plants are drawing on food stored from the previous year. If they are closely cropped early on, they lose vigor. If this is repeated for several years, they will die. Grazing in the middle of the season or later doesn't damage the grass.

Some high altitude areas have a very short growing season and the grass is young even at the peak of summer. Avoid grazing in such fragile, alpine areas. When packing into such country, bring your own horse feed. Pellets are the best type of feed because the pelletizing process destroys any weed seeds that might be in the feed. It is very important not to introduce any weeds or other foreign plants into the back-country environment.

Native weeds are seldom a problem because they fit into the environment and do not tend to take over and dominate the plant community. Weeds introduced from other areas can crowd out the native vegetation. Carrying seeds of noxious weeds to a horse camping area where they might take hold should be avoided. The possibility of introducing an unwanted plant from the horse feed is much greater at lower altitudes than it is higher up. Very few species of plants survive at high altitudes, and if a viable seed did escape, it would not reproduce. This

is also true in heavily timbered and semi-arid areas.

Pellets are closely compacted and contain both hay and grain, which reduces the bulk to be packed and makes the feed highly digestible. I carry about one pound of feed per hundred-weight of horse for one day. Thus I carry 250 pounds of feed for five horses weighting 1,000 pounds each for five days.

Horse campers should take along some pellets or "catchin' oats" even if grass is abundant. Feeding the horses every day will make the camp seem like home to them. If a horse is shy about being caught, it can be bribed with a handful of grain or pellets.

Horses must be accustomed to the feed they will get on the ride, or they might get colic from the sudden change. If a horse is getting baled hay, but will get pasturage or pellets on the ride, the new feed should be introduced gradually before the ride. Always avoid graining a hot horse, and don't water it for an hour after feeding.

7. Preparation

ONE AUTUMN, I was scheduled to pack Don Marshall and a party of friends from Texas into our elk hunting camp. The plan was to rendezvous at the trailhead at noon in order to have time to make camp before nightfall. A week before, I had packed my dad and his guests into the camp and had returned to the office. Now, I was back at the trailhead waiting. As arranged, my dad and his group packed out in the morning and arrived at the trailhead with plenty of time to rest the pack string before we turned them around and went back in. The only problem when they arrived was that the string was one horse short. Two days earlier, Ole Blue was packing the front quarters of a bull elk to camp and his pump quit. He was eighteen years old and passed on doing something he did well.

At four o'clock, my tardy Texans arrived with a mountain of personal belongings and a truckload of good things to eat and drink. They had volunteered to bring all the food if I would pack them in. My problem was that they were four hours behind schedule and I had to get their gear cargoed and packed, and then ford the group across the Lochsa River before dark.

Quickly, I had to trim their pile of goodies down to a size I could handle with my smaller-than-expected pack string. They had a box of apples and a crate of oranges. Now, there is a limit to how many oranges and apples four people can eat in seven days. They admitted that one each per day would be sufficient, and the rest of the fruit stayed behind. I reduced their liquid refreshment by a case and left out some loaves of bread and canned goods. In true Texas fashion, they had brought supplies for a month.

While the Texans got acquainted with saddle horses and adjusted their stirrups, I feverishly sorted out surplus groceries and cargoed packs.

We forded the river a few minutes before dark, but we still had a long, black night on the trail ahead of us. We didn't arrive at camp until after midnight.

It is not a good idea to wait until you are at the trailhead to assemble and cargo your gear and food. However, if you group is going to camp overnight at the trailhead before getting on the trail, then the campers will be using their eating and sleeping equipment before it is loaded on the horses. In such cases, you will have to wait until the morning to prepare most of the loads.

You will be able to cargo (package gear for tying onto a packhorse) all of your pack loads ahead of time if you have a short (half-day or less) road trip to the trailhead. Horses can even be saddled prior to loading them into the trailer. Then, as soon as the party reaches the trailhead, you can unload the horses, cinch up, pack them, and be on your way.

Get your party together the evening before departure and cargo the material that will be packed. Such preparation will save you a lot of time and effort at the trailhead.

ORGANIZATION

I F THE NUMBER of bags is kept to a minimum, there is much less confusion when you arrive at the first camp. It helps to mark the owner's name on his duffel bag. If each duffel bag is marked with its weight, it is easier to balance the loads on the packhorses. Once the distribution of packs is decided, you can mark the duffels with a different letter for each horse.

Remember—or better yet—mark which horse has the kitchen equipment and grub. Then, when you get to camp, it can be unpacked first and dinner can be started. Horse campers' dispositions improve drastically if they can be fed in short order after reaching camp.

Plan a timetable for loading up, leaving home, and arriving at the trailhead. Keeping to it will give the expedition an atmosphere of order and a feeling of confidence that the situation is under control. The planning has been done, information gathered, and there is no mystery concerning where the trip is going or for how long. When allotting time for different jobs, allow more time than you really think it will take. You'll probably need it.

If your plan is to drive to the trailhead and pack in all in one day, everything must click perfectly or you will be setting up camp in the dark. If you are meeting an outfitter at a certain time, plan to be there an hour or two early. Being late can work a severe hardship.

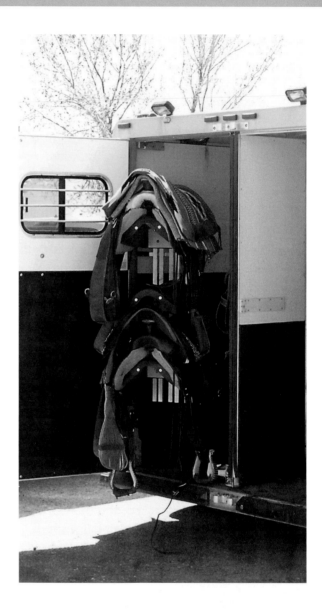

THE TERM "CARGOING" probably came into use about the time the Decker packsaddle was developed. Cargoing is the process of making packs of all the food, tents, beds, clothes, and other gear into a shape that can be tied onto the horses.

In cargoing a camp outfit, it is necessary that each pack is of manageable size and shape, and that it weigh about 75 pounds. Check the weight with a bathroom scale. While there can be some variation in the size and shape of packs, the best pattern to follow is that of a 50- to 60-pound bale of string-tied hay, twice as long as it is wide. Keep flat the side of the pack that lies next to the horse. If it is round, the pack will tend to rock back and forth.

Spread a manty out on the ground and have your cargo ropes handy. The gear to be cargoed is laid out diagonally in the center of the manty. Use a mixture of light and heavy articles. A finished pack of just light articles will be too bulky, and one of just heavy articles will be too small.

Adjust the items in each manty in order that their shapes help hold the pack together. For example, a metal fishing rod case laid alongside several small cardboard boxes will give a pack stability. Remember that articles in the pack will rub against each other as the horse walks. Do not have one article in the pack that will damage the others. A fence tool should not be packed next to an air mattress.

After articles have been selected for the pack according to shape, size, weight, and compatibility, the next step is wrapping them up. Figure out which end of the pack will be up. Be aware of anything that must remain upright. The heavier items should be at the top as the weight is carried better over the bars of the saddle rather than at the bottom end of the pack.

With the top end selected and the gear properly piled on the manty, fold the sides in, the bottom up, and top down (Figure A). By having the top fold on the outside, rain won't run into the pack.

The manty is then tied around the gear much like a Christmas package. Loop the cargo rope around the pack with the eye (or honda end) of the rope about one foot from the top end of the pack. Thread the other end of the rope through the eye and pull it tight toward you (Figure B). Make one half hitch around the pack below the eye and pull it snug (Figures C and D). Repeat this at the center of the pack, and again around the bottom quarter (Figure E). Run any extra rope around the pack endwise and tie it off (Figures F and G).

The purpose of the manty and the cargo rope is to package the cargo, hold it together, and protect it. If most of the articles you have are long, put the very first loop sideways around the top quarter, do half hitches at the center and bottom quarter, and then pull the end of the rope around the pack lengthwise, tying it off at the top.

Cargoing sawbucks is a matter of fitting all your gear, except your tents and sleeping bags, into a balanced pair of panniers. The sleeping bags, foam pads, and tents will be packed on top of the panniers once they are on the horses.

TYING THE MANTY

A.

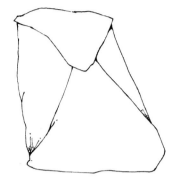

B.

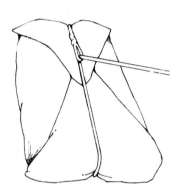

C.

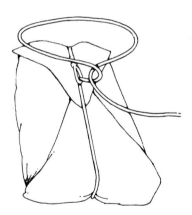

D.

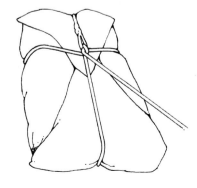

E.

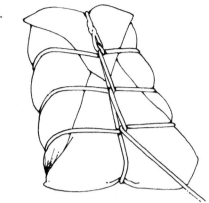

F.

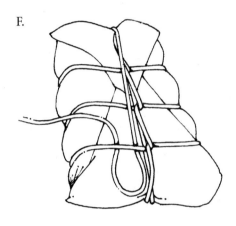

G.

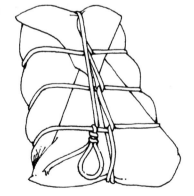

PACKS

I N HORSE CAMPING, packs are the two bundles of cargo that are tied on opposite sides of the Decker packsaddle. Time and effort can be saved if members of the party carry their personal gear, extra clothing, and sleeping bag in a duffel bag or navy sea bag. These bags should hold everything you need, except your tent.

Duffel bags weigh about forty pounds each when filled. Two of them can be mantied together into a single pack of eighty pounds. If the duffels are first cinched together tightly with some twine, and then laid side by side diagonally on a manty, they make a good pack of convenient size and shape. Tie up the manty with the loop around the two bags, which will make a tighter pack than putting the rope lengthwise.

If liquid fuel (white gas) is being packed for a stove or lantern, place it in a plastic jug or gallon can and tape the cap on. Pack the gas in the same pack as the stove, lantern, and other gear that will not be damaged if the gas spills. Keep the gas on a separate horse, away from the food or kitchen equipment.

Slip the ax and shovel under the cargo rope on the outside of the pack and tie the down

with a short rope or cargo rope end. Then, if the ax and shovel are needed to clear obstructions on the trail, they will be handy. If there is a lot of chopping to do, carry the ax on the lead saddle horse. Most forests require that pack outfits carry an ax, shovel, and bucket in case of forest fire.

GRUB BOXES

RUB BOXES specially made to pack on a Decker are taller than they are wide. They have a cleat on each side, which helps keep them positioned correctly on the saddle. The sling rope fits just beneath the cleats.

This type of grub box has a shelf in the center, which doubles the floor space. The shelf makes it possible to pack heavy items on the floor and on the shelf, and to pack lighter items on top of the heavier ones. Fill a pair of grub boxes at the same time in order to equalize weight. If one is completely filled first, and then the other, it is easy to get all the heavy items in one and the light, bulky items in the other. When the grub boxes are about three-quarters full, start hefting them to determine if they weigh the same. At home you can put them on a bathroom scale and make certain that they have equal weight. It is very important to have the grub boxes balanced.

The Decker grub box has a lid that is hinged on the bottom. In camp, this lid is folded out and used as an additional flat area for food items. On one of my grub boxes, a ¼-inch plywood sheet the same size as the box is fastened with wood screws to the back of the box. When unscrewed, this sheet can serve as a table top. A piece of sheet iron is fastened on the back of the other box for use as a stove top.

Grub boxes for sawbucks are wider than they are high. Mine are 18 inches by 24 inches by 12 inches, which is a little too wide. They would fit a horse better and not protrude so far on each side if they were curved on the side next to the horse. The sawbuck grub boxes do not usually have shelves, and if set up in camp on the side that was next to the horse face down on the ground, it is necessary to repack its contents. Setting it up in this fashion, however, does provide the most level space on which to set things.

After a meal is served, the lids of the grub boxes should be closed. This keeps out chipmunks, squirrels, white-footed mice, insects, and anything else (besides bears) that wants a free meal.

When packing the grub boxes, remember that any metal that touches other metal can make noise and/or can wear. Use newspapers or paper toweling between canned or bottled goods and have everything snugly packed. Screw tops should be turned tight and then taped with masking or cellophane tape. Eggs are not that difficult to pack. They need to be on the very top of the box. Wad some paper up and wedge it in between the cartons and the box top to prevent any bouncing around. Don't buy large eggs. They will be squeezed too much by the carton. Use medium-sized eggs and wrap a square of toilet tissue around each one. I do not recall ever arriving in camp with a broken egg. I maintain this record by packing the eggs snugly, as indicated above, and by packing the grub box on the most foolproof horse I own. I have had a few wrecks with packhorses, but never with the "kitchen horse."

Do not pack the soap in the same box with the food, and never pack cooking gear empty. Fill the kettles and coffee pot with food items or something else to prevent rattles and wear.

Laurence Hayer once made a set of grub boxes that looked too fancy to use. He used 3/8-inch AB plywood, more than 100 screws, and oak cleats. The corners were rounded off, and each box was carefully sanded before being coated with three layers of polyurethane. Each box had two lids that folded out to serve as shelf space. The lids were supported by ¼-inch nylon cord holding them at right angles to the box when they were folded out. The box size was 10 inches by 17 inches by 24 inches. If Hayer's grub boxes had a fault, it would be that they were so solidly constructed that if a horse ever rolled wearing a pair of them, it would likely break a few ribs.

Manty the grub box regardless of whether it will be packed on a Decker or sawbuck saddle. The manty will protect the box from dust, rain, and scrapes against rocks and trees.

8. Horse Hauling

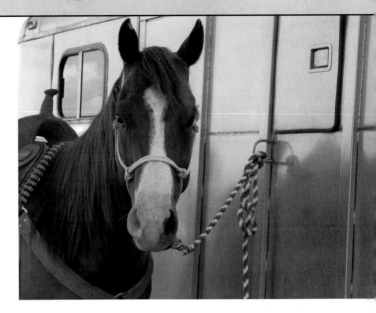

TRANSPORTING HORSES and horse campers to the trailhead can be a smooth, trouble-free experience, providing the vehicles are properly equipped and maintained. Most groups will have two or more vehicles, and those should travel as a convoy. Then, if one vehicle has a problem, the other can help solve it.

If no one in the party has been to the trailhead before, make certain that you have maps, and pay attention to the signs. Making a wrong turn on backcountry roads can get you lost, and there won't be anyone around to set you straight. Find out where you are going ahead of time, rather than en route.

All preparations for the trip should be made before the horses are loaded. Once the horses are loaded, the vehicles should move out. Horses don't like to be loaded and then made to stand in an enclosed area—which amounts to a horse straightjacket—while a half-hour's worth of last minute preparations are made. They will become impatient, and will paw, bite, or kick. So be sure to have air in the tires, the fuel tank filled, and the coolant and oil checked before the horses are loaded.

You won't know how a horse reacts to hauling until you have taken it on a trip. Most horses accept travel and do not cause any problems. There are ways to solve hauling problems when they develop. If a horse persists in pawing, put hobbles on its front feet. If a horse feels compelled to bite, put a nosebag or cavesson strap over its nose. Horses can sometimes be tied short enough to be prevented from biting other horses.

Like people, horses are compatible with some of their own kind and not with others. Load compatible horses, not feuding horses, next to one another.

Horse hauling goes slower than a business trip in a company car. If you allow enough time

you won't be tempted to drive fast. Shift into low gear for downhill grades. Horses create a top-heavy load. Their added weight calls for extra distance when stopping the vehicle. While hauling the horses, there should be ample time to think ahead some distance down the road.

If you have to stop, leave your vehicle in park or in first gear. Draw the emergency brake, and either block the wheels or turn them against a curb or obstacle. I knew of an Idaho couple who left their rig in the mountains to look at the view. When they returned, they discovered that it had rolled down the slope and overturned. One horse had to be destroyed. The movement of horses in a truck or trailer can start it rolling if it is not secured.

Check out health and brand requirements when transporting your horses across state and national boundaries. Many states require a current (within thirty days) health certificate, and some states and Canada require a Coggins test. Western states ask for a brand certificate, whether or not the horse is branded. If your horse is registered, carry a photocopy of the registration certificate. If not, take along a bill of sale. You might need to prove ownership.

EQUIPMENT

Y OUR CHOICE of what equipment to use to haul horses depends upon how many horses you will take. For a solo trip, you could get by with a two-horse trailer or a three-quarter-ton pickup with stock racks. Two people need a four-horse trailer, and three people will need a trailer large enough for six horses. Larger parties need two four-horse trailers or a stock truck with an eighteen-foot stock rack.

The topography of the country to be traveled will influence your decision concerning hauling equipment. Automatic transmissions and low horsepower (under the hood) might get the job done in flat country, but won't be sufficient in the mountains. For hauling horses on steep roads, a four-speed stick shift is necessary, and four-wheel drive is desirable. A truck with a two-speed rear axle does well in steep country, as it has the power and low gears to climb the hills and the low gears to use on descents.

Big diesel tractor-trailer outfits are not suited for moving horses on backcountry roads because these roads are often narrow with very sharp curves. Many trailheads don't have the unloading facilities and turnarounds for such rigs. My own horse hauling equipment consists of a four-horse trailer, a three-quarter-ton pickup with four speeds and four-wheel drive, a stock truck with twenty-two-foot rack, and a diesel tractor with forty-six-foot trailer. I have never used the diesel tractor on a horse-packing trip.

Supplemental equipment would include a tow cable or chain, jumper cables, and plastic jug or two full of water. A half-gallon of water poured over a hot radiator core will cool it down after a long climb. Don't shut off the motor, and keep the water off the fan. Rough mountain roads call for extra spare tires. Extra cans of motor oil and brake fluid are wise precautions against emergencies.

TRAILERING

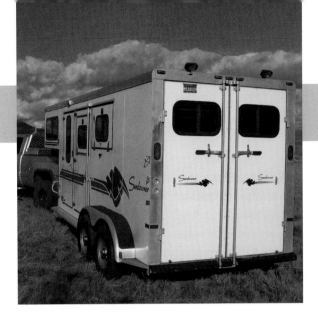

CHECK OVER THE TRAILER thoroughly some time before departing. A trailer needs a license, brakes, spare tire, tire changing equipment, taillights, reflector, stoplights, turn signals, a very sound hitch, and a safety chain. Check the tires, pack the wheel bearings, and make sure that the trailer floor is solid.

If you are hauling from some distance, pad the front of the trailer where the horse's chest and knees come into contact with the walls. Horses being hauled in two-, three-, or four-horse trailers are usually tied side by side, facing forward at an angle. A horse can brace itself a little better for forward and backward movement than for sideways movement. Compared to cattle, horses are top-heavy animals to haul. Take care when trailering to avoid making fast turns or quick starts and stops.

When turning with a trailer, do so slowly and don't accelerate before the trailer is straight. If you do, you'll whiplash the trailer. Take your foot off the gas before going into a curve on a crooked road. This will allow the horse to regain its balance. Poor driving causes horses to fight the trailer. One of the best ways to understand what the horse feels in the trailer is to ride in one pulled by an inconsiderate driver.

Trailers are attached to towing vehicles in two ways. I prefer a gooseneck hitch attached to the bed of the vehicle instead of a rear bumper hitch. A trailer on a gooseneck hitch is easier to control on the road and will often survive an emergency that would throw a trailer on a bumper hitch. The gooseneck reduces fishtailing, provides the stability for a comfortable ride for the horse, and allows the trailer to be turned in a smaller area. The gooseneck does reduce the hauling space in the pickup bed, a loss that can be compensated for by building storage space into the overhang part of the trailer.

Center partitions in some trailers extend all the way to the floor, which may cause horses to fight the trailer because they want to spread their feet further apart for better balance.

Horses need good air circulation, especially in hot weather. Keep all the vents open when moving and whatever doors and windows are feasible when stopped. Horses generate considerable heat and moisture by their breathing and sweating, which is increased by their coping with the movement of the trailer. In hot weather, tightly closed trailers can be ovens, and are even worse if they are painted with dark colors.

Load large trailers with most of the weight in front to keep the rig from fishtailing. A hay net full of hay should be provided for the horses on the road so that they have something to do and arrive at the trailhead well fed. Tie the hay net sufficiently high so that a horse can't get its front feet caught in it when the hay is half eaten.

Some owners like to unload their horses every six hours. If a horse refuses to urinate in the trailer, you will have to unload it. Horses can get some rest without being unloaded when the vehicle is stopped for fueling or for lunch. Watering the horses every six hours is a good idea, but the horses won't die if they refuse to drink. Many won't drink because the water offered on the road smells or tastes different from the water they have at home.

Don't overwork the horses immediately after a long trailer ride. Trailering can constrict blood vessels, and the horses will need a half-hour or so to return to normal.

TRUCKING

A TRUCK SHOULD HAVE the same checkup as a trailer before a trip. A truck, too, needs good brakes, legal lights, and a sound truck bed. Inspect the side racks for any nails, bolt, or other protrusions that could injure a horse.

In a pickup truck, the horses stand side by side facing forward. It helps if the rack is built to allow the horses to extend their heads over the cab, which puts more weight forward. Horses hauled in a pickup create a very top-heavy load, and extra care should be taken on curves and when stopping or starting.

It's much easier to haul horses in a one-and-a-half to three-ton truck, which provides a more stable platform than a pickup. The horses stand crosswise on the bed. This makes them more sensitive to sudden starts and stops, but also helps the horses manage curves better than if they are facing forward. Before the horses are loaded, make sure that the bank or loading dock is solid, and that there isn't any gap between the bed and the dock. A horse could be badly crippled by catching its leg in such a gap.

Load the first horse with its head to the right side of the truck and its rump to the left, and load the next horse facing the opposite way. This loading method makes optimum use of space and balances the load. As the horses are loaded, stretch a rope about a foot below the hip bones between each horse, or at least between each two horses. This gives the load more stability and prevents crowding. With the horses loaded crosswise, extra care must be taken when shifting. A sudden jerk will cause chaos.

When unloading, take care to have the tailgate tight against the unloading dock or bank. When there are only two horses left, get the last cross rope unfastened so that the last horse can come immediately following the next-to-last horse. This avoids fretting or pawing. Horses do get used to being hauled and will become more relaxed with experience.

TRAILHEAD

T HE TRAILHEAD is where the road ends and the trail begins, at least for your trip. The least improved trailheads have only a limited amount of parking. Of course, any parking is better than none. Unloading ramps for stock trucks are constructed by dozing dirt up to the plank wall of the correct height.

Some trailheads will have a pole saddling and packing chute made with round parallel poles about three feet off the ground and two-and-one-half feet apart. The horse is led in, tied, saddled, and packed while it is kept in one place by the poles. The best-equipped trailheads also have feeding and watering troughs, corrals, hitch racks, campsites, and toilets.

If you are going horse packing for the first time, try to find an improved trailhead. It will make your unloading, packing, and getting started much easier.

You'll find some good trailhead facilities that have deteriorated from weather and use. Help make the minor repairs that maintain horse facilities. Often a few shovels of dirt or a repaired pole will do wonders in showing the land managers that you appreciate the improvements and are trying to help maintain them. If you meet rangers, tell them that you used the trailhead facilities and appreciate them.

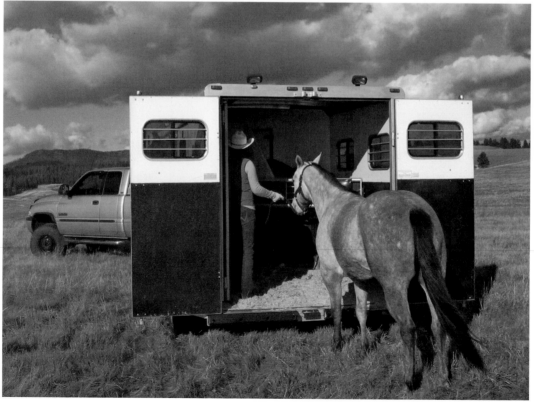

9. Trail Ready

I N 1948, JOE KING, his two brothers, and two friends went on a most enjoyable pack trip looking for elk around Greensides Butte in the Lochsa country of Idaho. They gave their outfitter, Buck Arp, a hand in packing the meat into camp and watched him attentively as he worked.

Two of the five-member party had ridden a fair amount, and they agreed to put together their own pack and saddle outfit for use the next fall. Well before the next elk season, they commissioned a friend who frequented the local sales barn to buy ten horses with the intention of riding half of them and packing the other half. At that time, the price of saddle and pack stock was much higher than the going rate for canners—the old, outlaw horses that should have been filling the nutritional requirements of cats and dogs. Ten head were bought.

The U.S. Cavalry had just been discontinued, and the Army was selling off thousands of McClellan saddles at reasonable prices. King and his group bought some saddles as well as sling and cargo rope, and manties. They loaded up their grub, camp, and newly acquired horses, and headed for the mountains. Being trusting souls, they thought that if someone had once used those horses as pack and saddle stock, then that was what they would be. They didn't bother with the formality of riding or packing them prior to the trip.

The end of the road and the beginning of the trail was three miles downstream from the Lochsa Ranger Station. Their destination was Surprise Creek. The surprise came when they tried to pack and ride their band of renegades. Joe recalled, "One time we had nine of those ten horses rolling down the mountain at the same time. It took us all day to cover the three miles to the ranger station. The next day we made six miles, and the third day we covered the last ten miles to Surprise Creek. By that time, the horses were getting broke, and we had learned a lot about packing."

They harvested five elk, packed out the meat, and went back after their camp. They went home and replaced seven of the ten horses, bought some packsaddles, and came back the next year all "trail ready." They went on to enjoy many fabulous trips. "One morning," Joe said, "I bugled, and eight different bulls answered." The bugle of a bull elk is one of the most wild, spine-tingling sounds I know.

Years later, Joe and his wife had only one week's vacation. They loaded up five horses, spent a day driving to the mouth of Boulder Creek, a day packing in, a day hunting (taking two elk), a day in camp, a day packing out, and another day driving home. Their friends had trouble believing that they could get that much done during their one-week vacation. What made it possible was being trail ready—taking care of all the details well in advance.

HOME PREPARATION

BEING TRAIL READY means having already done everything possible to prepare for a smooth, trouble-free trip. The more preparation done at home, the less that will have to be done at the trailhead. For example, the pack-saddle, harness, and latigos can be adjusted to the horses at home, and each horse's name can be written on the saddle that it will carry. This saves time at the trailhead. If the horses have never been packed before, it is much better to get them used to being packed at home by having them carry a couple of sacks of oats, rather than teaching them to carry a pack in the trailhead parking lot. These packing sessions at home can be as helpful to a first-time horse camper as they are to the first-time packhorse.

Some horses will show resentment at the sheer size of their load. Once they accept carrying two 75-pound sacks of oats, they can graduate to carrying two mantied packs consisting of two string-tied, 60-pound bales of hay each. After becoming relaxed and comfortable with the hay, the horses are ready for a pack trip.

After the vehicles are unloaded at the trailhead, they should be parked in the designated parking area or in a place where they will not block access to loading, watering, or feeding facilities. Park your vehicles close together, roll up the windows, take out the keys, lock the doors, and block the wheels if the rigs are parked on a slope.

Saddle your horse some time before starting on the trail. This allows the horse to become accustomed to its saddle and packsaddle harness, and to warm up the saddle blanket before being loaded. A saddle which is cinched snugly will often seem very loose thirty minutes later, even though the horse has stood still the entire period. A little interval between the time that the horses are saddled and the time they are packed makes cinching better.

Saddling begins with cleaning the horse's back. A quick brushing with a curry comb and brush will do the job. The blanket for the packsaddle is a thick, quilted pad that is longer than the pads used with riding saddles. Place the pad with its center on the middle of the horse's back. It will be correctly positioned when it appears to be two or three inches too far forward.

The breeching on a packsaddle is between the forks, and the breast collar is run through the front fork, through the cinch ring, over the breeching, and under the rear fork. The saddle should be placed with the bars fitted up just behind the shoulder blades, which is where it is made to sit. If it is too far forward, the front of the bars will protrude out from the horse. If it is too far back, there will be a space between the bars and the shoulder blades. There should be two or three inches of saddle pad in front of the half-breed boot. Since the horse's hair lies back, the saddle pad is more likely to slide backward than forward.

Remove the breast collar from the cinch ring, make certain the latigo and cinch are straight, and cinch the saddle. You should be able to put your hand under the fastened breast collar. The breeching is let down over the hips, and the quarter strap is hooked to the cinch ring. Pull the horse's tail over the breeching. You should be able to slide your hand under the breeching. If it is too tight, it will rub every time a step is taken and will eventually cause a gall.

The weight and content of the packs will determine which horses will carry them. The heavier packs will go on the older, bigger, or tougher horses. The light ones will go on the younger horses. Determine which are the most reliable horses and load the most fragile items (included food and cooking equipment) on them. The horses that do not want to be packed should be loaded with indestructible items such as feed, duffel, and sleeping bags.

Packing Up—Decker

Packing a horse is the process of securing the packs to the packsaddle. Most packs to be carried on a Decker will be tied on with a crowfoot hitch, which is actually an extension of the basket hitch. While most packs would get to their destination using the basket hitch, they will be more stable with the crowfoot. The cinch should be retightened just before packing. When the load is placed on the saddle, the weight will press the bars of the saddle into the thick pad and loosen the cinch. Therefore, pull the cinch tighter on a packsaddle than on a riding saddle. What appears to be tight prior to packing can be too loose after packing. One person can pack a horse, but it is much easier for two people.

Move the horse to the pair of packs it is to carry. Tie it up or have it held. Because most horses are mounted from the left side, they are easier to pack by starting from that side.

To tie a crowfoot:

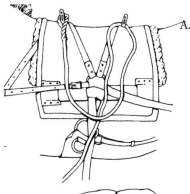

A. Take down the sling rope and make certain that it goes through the back fork from the rear. Pull the rope out from between the two forks to make somewhat more slack available than will be needed to go around the pack.

B. Lift the pack up and place it on the saddle with top up and the flat side against the saddle. It should be lifted high enough for the sling rope to be pulled across the middle of the upper half of the pack. Pull the slack rope over the pack and tighten enough to hold the top half of the pack against the saddle. Rock the pack back and forth several times while keeping pressure on the rope.

C. Bring the rope under the center of the pack and then up to that part of the rope that went across the pack. Keep the rope tight and force a small loop of the rope behind and under the rope that goes across the top of the pack.

D. A large loop from the end of the rope is then forced through this small loop.

E. The small loop is then pulled tight.

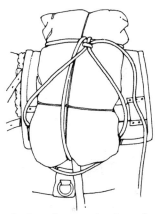

F. Enlarge the large loop so that it can be passed around the sides of the pack.

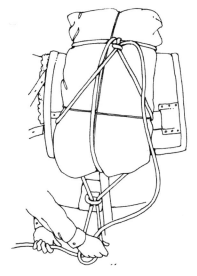

G. Pass the bottom of the loop through the tie-down ring. The free end of the rope is passed through the part of the loop that is sticking through the tie-down ring.

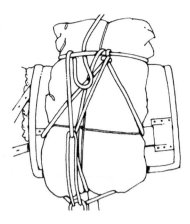

H. Pull upward. This will take the slack out of the rope holding down the sides of the pack. Take the free end of the rope up to the top rope and again force a small loop behind and under.

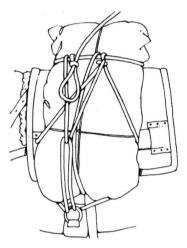

I. As before, pull a loop from the free portion of the rope through the small loop and draw it tight.

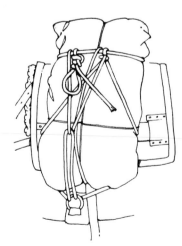

J. Use the free end of the rope to make two half hitches around the remaining loop.

If someone is handy to support the weight of the first pack on the horse, his support will keep it from unbalancing the horse and pulling the saddle down to one side.

Move to the horse's other side and tie on the other pack. If there is plenty of sling rope left, it can be placed over the top of the packs, run through the loop that was half-hitched, drawn snug, and tied off with two half hitches. If there is not enough rope to reach the other side, a small loop can be made in the rope's end using a bowline, and the free end of the rope from the other side can be passed though the loop, drawn snug, and half-hitched. The various loops and half hitches make unpacking quick and easy. All that is necessary for unpacking particularly fast is to take out the half hitches and pull.

Another hitch that is suited for a very long pack is the post hitch (or barrel hitch). For this hitch, the sling rope is pulled forward through the font fork to make a loop larger than the pack. Then a loop is pulled out and dropped behind and below the rear fork, leaving the free end forward in front of the rear fork. The front of the pack is placed inside the front loop, which is pulled snug. The back loop is placed around the back end of the pack and the free portion of the rope is pulled tight. The free end of the rope is then pulled under the center of the pack, up to the portion of the rope between the forks, and is tied off in the same manner as the crowfoot hitch.

barrel hitch

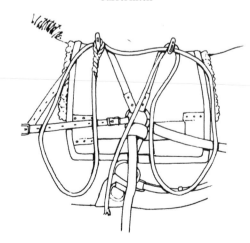

If the pack string is almost packed, and someone discovers some duffel that was overlooked, it can be top-packed. Place the duffel between the two packs and between the forks of the saddle. Tie the free end of the sling rope from the left pack to the front fork, leaving enough slack for the rope from the right pack to be passed under the left rope, pulled back, run under the back fork, and finally pulled snug and tied with two half hitches. The ropes should form a cross on the top center of the pack. To pack a foam pad, tie the end of an eight- or ten-foot rope to the front fork, and make a loop around the end of the pad. Pull the free end back under the front fork, under the back fork, around the rear of the pad, and then under the back fork. Tie it off on the front fork.

PACKING UP—SAWBUCK

With a sawbuck packsaddle, the beginner can pack all of his equipment in panniers, hang the panniers on the sawbuck, and be done with it. Panniers have the disadvantage of being limited in size and capacity to carry bulky or heavy items.

When panniers are used, sleeping bags and tents will often be packed on top. A sleeping bag can be laid on each side of the cross bucks with a small duffel in the center. Another horse could carry foam pads on each side, a duffel in the center, and a tent on top. Because top packs tend to be top-heavy, pack only light gear on top, and balance the panniers.

The loose gear piled on top of the panniers needs to be protected from the weather and secured to the rest of the pack. A pack cover or manty should cover the pack and be secured by a diamond hitch to hold everything in place. The easiest diamond hitch to remember is the "one-man diamond." To tie it:

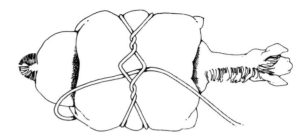

B. Twist the ropes at the top center of the pack twice. Bring the free part of the rope up from the ring and around the lower center-rear of the right pannier.

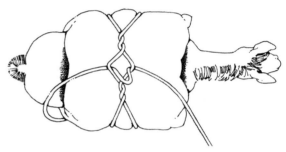

C. Pull a loop of rope through the center of the twist and lay the free end of the rope over the front of the right pannier.

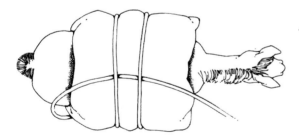

A. Pull a loop of rope through the ring end of the last inch and, with the free end of the rope laid across the pack from tail to head, throw the cinch over the center of the pack. Pull the hook end of the cinch up under the horse and hook it in the loop. Pull the free end of the rope snug.

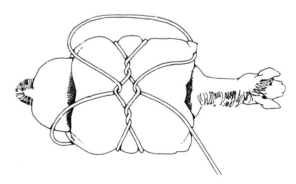

D. Enlarge the loop through the center twist, and pull the loop snugly around the lower rear of the left pannier and the lower front of the left pannier.

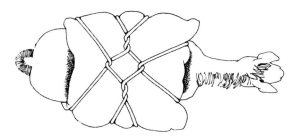

E. Pull the free end of the rope down snugly around the lower front of the right pannier.

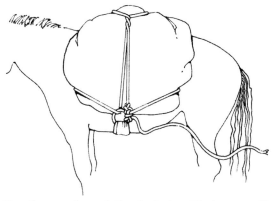

F. Run the rope through the cinch ring. Tie the rope off with two half hitches. This hitch works well when all slack is pulled out and the knot is tight.

In Idaho, the Decker packsaddle is used almost to the exclusion of the sawbuck. One autumn, I was visiting with an outfitter friend while several "do-it-yourself" parties were getting packed. One father and son party was busy packing its horses when the father spotted two old-timers putting a top pack on a sawbuck. He said, "Hey, those fellows are going to throw a diamond hitch." He grabbed his son and ran over to the old-timers so that his son could take a look. He was afraid that his son would never again have the opportunity to see that historic hitch used. He was unaware that sawbuck saddles are still used in many parts of the country, and that the diamond hitch is in no danger of extinction.

RIDING SADDLE

THE EASIEST WAY to pack a riding saddle is to purchase a pair of the canvas panniers ready-made for such saddles. These panniers are quite large and will accommodate bulky items. If a riding saddle is to be packed in steep country, use both a breaching and breast collar.

If you need to pack a riding saddle and don't have custom-made panniers, rig the saddle with sling ropes in much the same way as a Decker. Make two half hitches over the cantle at the center of a sixty-foot long 3/8-inch rope. Tie the saddle strings near the cantle around the rope. Pass the free end of the rope through the fork from the front. This arrangement works well on a high-backed, high-forked saddle. If a saddle has a low back and low fork, anchor the center of the rope to the horn with two half hitches, run the free end around the cantle, and tie loosely with the saddle strings. Pack the saddle as you would a Decker.

Hooking Up

Hook up your horses in the pack string with an eye for peace and harmony. Every horse will be more compatible with some horses than with others. You'll find some that seem to bear a grudge for another specific horse. Avoid hooking two together that want to fight. If a horse is particularly troublesome and bites other horses, put it in front. If a horse likes to kick, put it in the caboose. Choose a lead horse that is not spooky or squeamish about crossing wet spots, streams, or fallen logs. A reluctant horse will cooperate more readily if it is following a more confident leader. An over-eager horse can be controlled better in front than further back where it could cause problems by trying to pass the next horse in line.

If a horse is being packed for the first time, it is safer to lead it alone rather than in a string. Then, if the horse takes a little time getting used to its new role, it will not disrupt the others.

The longer the string of horses, the more opportunity there is for trouble. If the person leading the string does not slow down for sharp switchbacks and obstacles, there can be a crack-the-whip effect on the horses at the end of the string. A party of first-time campers with first-time horses would do well to make their strings as short as possible.

In most novice horse camping parties, there will be a member or two who will have a full-time job just keeping themselves and their riding horse on an even keel, without the added responsibility of leading a packhorse. People in this category should not be asked to lead a horse.

Horses can become irritable and impatient if they are hooked up and then have to stand around. Leave the packed horses tied up individually until just before hitting the trail. As soon as they are hooked up, leave.

To hook up one horse to another, double the end of the lead rope and put it through the loop at the end of the pigtail. Make a half hitch or two with the lead rope. Allow each horse enough rope for its nose to just barely reach the ground, starting from a point where the horse's head is level with the rear flank of the horse it is following. This length will allow the horse to drink when crossing a stream, but not to trip over the rope in its path or to pass another horse.

The lead rope, which the rider is holding, should have a loop at its end. Make a loop by putting a bowline in the rope's end. This will create a bail similar to the bail on a bucket. While holding onto the loop, if the lead packhorse stops suddenly or bolts, you will be less like to have the rope jerked out of your hand. You'll get a good jerk, but you won't lose the horse.

If you need to get off your horse, you can tie it up and lay the loop of the lead rope over the horn. Do not tie the lead rope to the horn or lead the string with the lead rope fastened to the horn.

10. On the Trail

DRIVER'S EDUCATION is taught to young people to help prevent auto accidents. They will never have to face all the problems studied in the course, but there is a recognized benefit for them knowing what can happen. Most accidents can be prevented by knowing how to prevent them.

This chapter on rider's education is written to help the first-time horse camper stay out of trouble. It is not my intention to convince anyone to abandon the idea of a pack trip. Quite the contrary. The trail, like the highway, can be source of problems, but most of them can be avoided. Those that cannot be prevented can be coped with.

Some of the challenges faced by new horse campers can be quite entertaining to the old-timers. Boulder Flats in the Bitterroot Mountains in Idaho has been a popular staging area for elk hunters since the highway was built to that point on the Lochsa River. A favorite spectator sport for packers is to watch the amateurs begin their trips into the mountains. There will always be enough beginners who don't know how to pack, and enough half-broke horses that don't want to be packed, to make it a great show. For some, the trailhead rodeo is only the beginning of a backcountry fiasco. Of course, the next time around, these amateurs will be old-timers themselves and can join in the laughter.

I had one trailhead mishap that would have gotten a laugh had there been any spectators. I had hung some big, wide, wooden boxes on a Decker saddle that I had placed on a horse that was inclined to pull back if something spooked it. Something did spook it as I started to untie it, and the horse pulled back hard. The snap on the lead rope broke and the horse went over backwards, with the boxes preventing it from rolling to either side. It was like a turtle on its back, with all four legs thrashing the air, and it took a lot of pulling with a lariat dallied (or turned) around the saddle horn to get the horse right side up.

Educating the horse at home will make using it on the trail easier. A trail horse should accept mounting and dismounting on either side. Horses that are used to being mounted and dismounted from both sides are much easier to pack and to work with if a pack needs to be retied.

Moving Out

BEFORE LEAVING THE TRAILHEAD, decide the riding order for your party. It is wise to have someone riding drag who is not leading a packhorse. His or her responsibility is to watch for dropped gear and loose packs. The drag can also catch loose horses if they become unhooked. Ben Jain said that after the Chief Joseph Trail Ride used the trail from Boles to the Salmon River, the local cowboys picked up enough cameras, binoculars, jackets, and slickers to outfit themselves for the next ten years.

Moving out should be slow at first to give the horses a chance to get used to their packs and to being hooked together. They need a little time to learn how to follow when the horse ahead moves out, and not to wait until they get a tug on the lead rope.

The riders who are leading horses should look back often during the first two or three miles to make certain that the horses are coming along well and that the packs are balanced. An unbalanced pack will often not be evident until the cinch begins to loosen a few miles up the trail. To watch for unbalanced packs, look at the forks of the packsaddle. If the fork is straight and not tilted to one side or the other, then the pack is balanced.

All riders should pay attention to how the packs are riding. If a pack begins to flop around or drop down, stop and retie it before it comes off. If a pack drops off, it usually spooks the horse, even if the horse is quite gentle.

REST STOPS

SET A SLOW PACE that the horses can handle rather than rushing along and then stopping to rest. Don't push the horses on steep trails; some are steeper than they look.

Inexperienced packhorses or horses from different owners are more apt to have a foul-up while resting than they are while moving along the trail. When stopped, horses will sometimes try to pass each other, rub against a tree, or bother each other.

Give the horses a good rest at lunchtime. As the party will be stopped for an hour or so, it is best to unhook the pack string and tie up the horses individually. Regroup the string again just before leaving.

A little break at mid-morning and mid-afternoon is good for both horses and riders. A rest stop gives horses an opportunity to urinate, which is particularly important for horses that are working hard. Resting helps prevent azoturia, or tying up. If the horses have heated up, don't stop for a rest on a windy ridge. A chilly wind on a hot horse increases its chance of developing azoturia.

Occasionally, a horse that has had an easy life will feel overloaded and try to lie down at a rest stop. Be sure that the horses are tied high enough on a short lead to prevent them from lying down.

The condition of the horses, the overall pace of the trip, the grade of the trail, the weight of the riders and packs, and temperature, humidity, and altitude all influence how many rest stops are needed. People are important, too. They should stop when they need to, regardless of what the horses think about it.

TRAIL RIDING

TRAIL RIDING IS DIFFERENT from arena riding in that conditions in the arena are fairly static. A horse will become accustomed to the unchanging atmosphere of the arena. In contrast, the trail and its surroundings on a pack trip present a constantly changing scene.

A horse will see, hear, and smell all sorts of strange things. These dramatic changes can unnerve a novice trail horse. The rider needs to pay attention to what is coming up next and be sensitive to how his horse will react.

Soon after cow cutting became popular in rodeos, some young people considered it fashionable to ride with very loose reins. After all, look what loose reins the cutting horse riders used and what perfect control they had. The loose reins proved to the judge that the horse was doing it all on its own.

Loose reins have no place in trail riding. A rider should be in contact with his horse at all times. A rider with a foot of slack in his reins is riding a loose horse. If spooked, the horse can turn out from under the rider before the foot of reins can be gathered up to bring the horse under control.

Horses soon become accustomed to most of the new things that they find on a pack trip. Many will become as interested in the adventure as the people they serve. In most groups of horses, there will be one that is unaffected by even the most terrifying sights and sounds. Have that horse lead the group. Horses are enough like sheep to follow.

CROSSING STREAMS

Most pack trips in mountain country involve stream crossings. If your horse was raised in the backyard drinking out of an automatic waterer, it should be exposed to water before facing a stream crossing. Find a low spot, stand your horse in it, and fill it with a garden hose. Walk the horse around in the water, turn the garden hose on its legs, and expose it to water until it becomes accustomed to it.

Stream crossings are a good place to give the horse a drink. If the stream is small, let your saddle horse and the lead packhorse drink. Then move them forward to make room for the next horse or two to drink. Keep this up until the whole string has had a drink, and then move on. If you give a hot horse a cold drink (and most stream water is cold), you should move on to prevent the horse from getting a stomachache.

Horses can easily ford streams that are knee high. If the water is swift and belly high, it can turn a horse a little sideways. If the stream is cold, swift, and deeper than belly high, don't try to ford it. The size of the rocks in the stream is also important. If the rocks are the size of three-pound coffee cans, they are no problem. If they are the size of kitchen stoves, they can cause the horse to flounder about. Use as a lead horse one that is accustomed to crossing streams.

If you are crossing a cold mountain stream with hot horses, give them a drink of water, but do not stop in the stream for long. The cold water can cause muscle cramps, which in turn might cause your horses to collapse. The only horse lost on the 1974 100-mile, one-day Tevis Ride from Squaw Valley to Auburn, California, was lost because the rider rode out into the American River and let the horse stand too long in the cold water. It went down, and although a good equine veterinarian quickly attended it to, it did not respond to treatment.

BOOGERS

A BOOGER IS ANYTHING that frightens a horse. An unfamiliar environment will contain a number of objects that horses will shy away from. While horses are not bothered by rocks smaller than a basketball or larger than a refrigerator, it is amazing how strongly they will react to a rock two feet square. This is particularly true if the rock has recently rolled down a mountain. Bears often move chunks of timber while looking for food. Horses shy away from such chunks, either because they resent having the wood moved, because it looks unnatural to them, or because there is still some bear scent around.

My pack string once was alarmed when it met a half dozen small Boy Scouts carrying huge packs. The horses must have thought they were little green Martians. Another time, I met a hiker accompanied by an enormous black Labrador carrying a light brown pack on its back. My horses were certain it was a grizzly bear.

If you see a booger in time, avoid it. If possible, give it the right-of-way. When a horse panics and can be controlled better from the ground, get off. Keep a strong hold on the lead rope and don't get yourself stepped on or run over. A loose, frightened horse can tear up equipment or injure itself.

Sometimes horse campers create their own runaways. If one of the riders suddenly gets the urge to take a brisk canter, remember that the other horses will want to join the fun.

HAZARDS

Any obstacle that causes danger is a hazard, regardless of whether it frightens the horses or not. Tree limbs can brush a rider's hat off or slap him in the face. In early spring in the Rockies, there are wood ticks. A few of them carry Rocky Mountain spotted fever, which can be quite dangerous. Now the fever can be treated successfully and is no longer a problem if taken care of promptly.

When a yellow jacket nest is close to the trail, they can get aggravated and sting the horses on the legs. The ensuing panic can break pigtails and send horses stampeding in all directions. Deerflies are a bother but don't cause the trouble that horseflies do with their bites.

Bogs are another hazard. Some trails go through places with very soft, wet soil, and a horse can have quite a struggle. Once, Bob Peckinpah rode his horse through a boggy spot and the horse sank until Bob's stirrups touched the mud. Bob stepped off, which is easy when your stirrups are at ground level. Relieved of his weight, the horse pulled itself out.

Beginning horse campers should avoid trails that are hazardous. The trail up the Selway River in Idaho climbed high over a 500-foot, sheer drop called Tepee Bluffs. Before the trail was rebuilt on a water grade near the river, thirty head of pack stock lost their lives there.

Rolling rocks can also be dangerous. Fortunately, most of the rock comes loose in the early spring before campers come into the backcountry. Often, a falling rock will cause enough noise to warn those below. Don't roll rocks for entertainment; there could be a person downhill from you.

TRAFFIC RULES

THE RULES FOR right-of-way on trails are generous to the horseman. Both hikers and motorcyclists are supposed to move to the side for horses. However, common sense and courtesy should take precedence over the rules. If it is easier for the pack string to move than a motorcycle, for example, then the pack string should yield. The best way for horsemen to assure their continued use of the trails is to bend over backward to be helpful and courteous to other users.

Usually, one pack string can step aside when meeting another pack string on the trail. However, once along the old Selway River trail, my dad and I met another pack string and it was impossible to pass one another. We had the shorter string. I was leading and my dad was following. After we stopped, Dad got off his horse and turned it around on the trail, with its head facing away from the bluff. Then, he unhooked the horse from the caboose

and turned it around. Each horse was then unhooked, turned around, and hooked again. I got off my horse, turned it around, and we went back for a hundred yards where we could stop and let the longer string pass.

Usually, traffic problems can be solved with a little communication. I once met a motorcycle near a rockslide, which prevented us from passing. The cyclist left his machine running, and my horses could not adjust to its sound, sight, or smell. In order to break the impasse, I got off my horse, walked down the trail to the cyclist, and explained to him that I had a string of backwoods horses that had never seen or heard a motorcycle before. If we were going to get by one another, he had to shut off his motor, and I would help him push the machine back on the trail to a point where we could pass. He was very agreeable. He wanted to help and only needed to know how. Most people in the backcountry are easy to get along with.

Trail Maintenance

BOTH HORSES AND RIDERS will have plenty of stops on a rarely used trail while members of the party work on trail maintenance. Horsemen are better equipped than hikers to do trail maintenance because they can carry an ax, shovel, and even a saw. Since the rider has been carried by a horse, he will have the energy to shovel out a dirt slide or chop a fallen tree lying across the trail. Getting off your horse and working on the trail adds variety to the trip and restores circulation to the backside.

Because government budgets for trail work are so low, land managers deeply appreciate the help they get from trail users. It used to be that official trail maintenance was done to enable government pack strings to supply backcountry lookouts for fire prevention. Now much of the supply work and fire patrol are done by airplane.

I never begrudge any time spent maintaining trails because I thoroughly enjoy the country I get to see from them. I deeply appreciate the privilege of using public land for a pack trip. Doing trail work is a way of saying "thank you" and improves public relations for horse users.

Finding the Way

I
F NO ONE IN THE PARTY is familiar with the trail, take a map or GPS. While many trails are well marked, sometimes signs are torn down by bears or taken away by people. Don't try to find your way by relying solely on signs.

Geological survey maps are marked off in squares of a determined distance, which is indicated in a table on the edge. You can use these squares to estimate mileage, but remember that the actual trail mileage will be greater than it appears to be from the map because of ups, downs, and curves in the trail. Some people swear that one map mile equals one-and-a-half real miles. One way to estimate distance is by keeping track of the time spent on the trail. In mountain country, a pack string will cover between three and three-and-one-half miles per hour.

You can often pinpoint your location on the map by identifying landmarks such as streams, lookout towers, switchbacks, and bends in the trail. By checking contour lines, it is usually possible to determine the relationship of the trail to ridges and drainages. The majority of trails follow the tops of ridges or the sides of streams. If the trail climbs a mountain, the map will indicate switchbacks.

Most backcountry trails are marked with blazed trees. Sometimes the streams are identified with signs, which helps in finding them on the map. Do not head off-trail across mountain or desert country without good maps. And if you do get confused, don't panic. Mountain men were in strange country their entire lives. Their equipment and food supply were not as good as yours, and you don't have to worry about unfriendly natives.

WILDLIFE

MOST PEOPLE LOOK FORWARD to seeing wildlife on their trips. It is exciting to watch mule deer bouncing away or elk feeding in a fern glade. Such sights are the rewards and bonuses of being on a pack trip. While horses pay little heed to deer, elk, and coyotes, they can't tolerate moose and will panic in meeting a bear. If a grouse flies up from under your horse, be prepared for it to shy or jump sideways.

Horse campers have the opportunity to see more game because a horse is another four-legged animal, and game is accustomed to seeing other animals. Enjoy the game, but don't chase, harass, or disturb them. You are a guest in their home. Deer and elk tend to feed in the morning and evening, and bed down during the middle of the day. They feed in partially open areas and glades where browse is available. They especially like the tender shoots of young brush that grows up following a burn.

Bighorn sheep are more nervous than deer and will bed down, get up and feed, and bed down again during the day. Antelope like open, semi-arid, sagebrush and grassland areas. They protect themselves by running away, not by hiding. If you ride through their area, you will see them.

Moose like to feed in small lakes and wet meadows. Unlike other animals, bear have no particular environment and can be seen any place, eating anything, at any time of day. They have excellent smell and hearing, and will stay out of sight if they know you are near. Cougars are rarely seen. Once considered a predator, they are now regarded as a big game animal that may be hunted only under strict controls.

Dogs are inclined to chase game and are best left at home. Wild animals add music to the pack trip. Sounds can be as memorable as sights. I vividly remember the howl of the wolf on a pack trip in northern British Columbia.

11. Setting Up

ONE AUTUMN, my dad and I didn't pack in for elk until mid-October. We hadn't hunted at Otter Butte before, and we didn't know what the country looked like. We had to cross the Selway River at a ford where the rocks were the size of automatic dishwashers. A long, slow climb put us at Otter Butte Lookout Tower well after dark. It had been raining at the river, but with the three-thousand-foot climb, there was a foot of snow. The only flat spot in the country seemed to be directly beneath the lookout tower. We unpacked, shoveled a lot of snow, set up our tent, and tied the horses in some thick timber. Our hands were freezing from working with the wet, cold ropes.

When we could see the country the next morning, we moved camp about one-half mile into a flat saddle, where we would be out of the wind. Elk were plentiful, and we were packing out in two days. Another foot of snow fell. Two feet of snow might be great for ski camping, but it is certainly not great for horse camping.

The normal procedure for setting up camp can be unexpectedly delayed. On one trip, a guest from California, Lyle Golden, a fine carpenter, was very handy in setting up our two tents and the kitchen area between them. As soon as we rode into the camping area, he dismounted, dropped his reins, and started getting poles fixed for the tents. His overfed and hot horse immediately headed for the creek and drank a bellyful of ice-cold water. I was busy unpacking horses and didn't see the loose horse go for the water, but I did hear it groaning and trying to roll. Abandoning camp, I started walking the sick horse so that the cold water in its stomach would warm up. After forty-five minutes of walking, the horse recovered. Don't let a hot horse drink cold water as soon as it arrives in camp.

The ideal camps are set up in good weather, in daylight, by people who have camped before. If the various jobs are efficiently carried out by experienced people, setting up camp can be as satisfying and exciting as moving into a new house at a picture-book location.

Every ship needs a captain. A party of novice campers might want to designate one of their members to take command and delegate duties. Arranging to have the supper cooked, horses cared for, and the tents set up all at one time saves work and time.

GEAR

THE CARE OF RIDING and packing gear is as important on the pack trip as it is at home. Lash a smooth pole between two trees to use as a long saddle rack for your gear. If no poles are around, use a fallen log. If there is no timber at all, stack the gear on the ground. Wherever it is stacked, the gear should be covered with a manty. Rocks or short poles can be used to keep the manty from being blown away. Hang wet saddle blankets over a rope or ropes where they can dry out. If it is raining, cover the blankets with the rest of the gear and let them dry when the rain quits.

Leaving gear lying around on the ground wherever it was unpacked can have serious consequences. L. W. "Bill" Moore suffered the consequences on a pack trip in the autumn of 1948. An outfitter packed him into Norton Ridge on the Middle Fork of the Salmon, arriving at camp after dark.

The sky was clear with no hint of a storm. The party was tired, and they didn't bother to set up tents. The outfitter was tired, and he let the gear drop where it was taken off the horses. He was very trusting of his string of saddle horses and pack mules, and turned them all loose.

At midnight, one of the party awoke to find it snowing. By daylight, there was a foot of snow on the ground. The pack string and saddle horses had left the country. The outfitter kicked around in the snow and eventually found a few halters and lead ropes. He set off on foot to find his stock.

The sleeping bags were soaked. The group set up tents, built a fire, and started drying out sleeping bags and duffel. The outfitter spent the greater part of the next week trying to locate his snow-covered gear, and after an extensive search, was still missing five head of stock.

LOCATION

THE MOST ESSENTIAL THING to look for in a camp location is drinking water. Water is necessary for both the campers and the horses. In some areas, the water may be contaminated by heavy use. If that is a possibility, use iodine, or boil the water to make it safe for people.

A camp needs enough level ground for pitching tents. Proper rest is impossible if your sleeping bag is rolling off your foam pad or air mattress.

Keep the horses in mind. Check the site for good grazing. If grazing is permitted, locate your camp within a reasonable distance from the grazing. The location should also avoid hazards such as dead trees that might fall over or areas subject to flash floods. Don't choose a site exposed to wind, which can uproot tent pegs and blow the manties off of staked gear.

Be aware of air drainage in the mountains. A camp in a very low meadow with poor air drainage will be cooler than a camp on a high bench with good air drainage. If you ride in hilly country some late autumn evening, you will find a dramatic difference in temperature. The ridges and benches will be warm and the draws and meadows will be cool.

UNPACKING

W HEN THE CAMPSITE has been located, tie the
horses on the perimeter of the site. Lead
the kitchen horse up to the area where the cooking will be done, and unpack it. As soon as the
horse that carries the food and cooking equipment is unpacked, tie up its sling ropes and take
the horse back to the perimeter. While some
members of the party prepare supper, others
can unpack the horses carrying duffel bags and
tents. Unpacking the horses one or two at a time
will reduce the amount of horse droppings that
have to be carried out of camp.

Let the horses' backs cool slowly after they
are unpacked. If the horses remain saddled for
at least thirty minutes after being unpacked,
they are much less likely to develop sore backs.
There are plenty of other things to do while the
horses are cooling.

Choose a place for the saddles to be stacked.
As the horses are unsaddled, stack up their
saddles. To unsaddle a packhorse from the near
side, unhook the lower quarter strap. Place
the tail under the breeching, lift the breeching
up and forward, and lay it between the forks.
Unbuckle the breast collar. Uncinch and run the

latigo back into the rigging ring. Move
to the off side, lift up the cinch, and
run the breast collar under the front
fork, through the cinch ring, over the
breeching, and under the rear fork. If
the horse is gentle when approached
from its off side, remove the saddle
from there—that saves moving back to
the near side to finish the job.

KITCHEN

GETTING THE KITCHEN located and set up quickly is important because the riders will be hungry from the trail. Situate the kitchen where there won't be a dust problem created by horse and people traffic. Try to find a place with sun in the morning and shade in the afternoon. The sun will make cooking and eating breakfast more pleasant, and the shade will keep the food cooler in the afternoon.

In the summer or spring, a fly over the cooking area will protect it from both sun and rain.

In the autumn, the kitchen needs to be entirely enclosed. The tent and kitchen arrangement that I use for late autumn hunting parties has a ten-foot, enclosed kitchen between two wall tents.

In the autumn, I use a homemade wood-burning stove that thoroughly heats the kitchen and takes the chill off the two tents. The grub boxes are set up about eight feet from the stove. This is close enough to be handy, but far enough away to protect the food from the heat.

PEOPLE

THE COMFORT OF THE GROUP will depend upon the number of hours spent in the saddle, and how soon the people can be fed when they arrive at camp. By reaching a campsite several hours before sundown, you can get the camp chores done and have supper ready before dark.

It takes some division of work to fetch water, cook supper, store gear, feed and/or graze horses, and put up tents. Fortunately, in a party of four or five campers, there will be a variety of interests and talents. There is always someone ready to cook and others willing to wrangle horses.

If everyone shares the work, and then helps someone else, the chores get done and no one is overworked. Chores that at home are classified as work become part of the fun of the camping experience.

Professional outfitters try to keep their clients comfortable by not having too many hours in the saddle, and by getting into camp well before sundown. While the outfitter will have a crew to do camp chores, they will usually accept assistance from members of the party who want to be helpful.

HORSES

WHAT TO DO WITH THE HORSES after they have been unsaddled depends upon the time of day. If there are two or three hours of daylight left and some good grazing nearby, two members of the group should graze the horses. Graze them until dusk, and then bring them back near camp to be tied up for the night. If there is no grazing available, feed the horses pellets or grain before turning in for the night.

If a few of the horses are broke to stake, they can be staked in a suitable place. Take care in selecting such a site. The ground should be firm and at least two hundred feet from any creek or

lake. Don't tie the horses to young trees, as the bark will be soft, and the lead shank will girdle the tree. The pawing of a nervous horse can damage tree roots. A picket line strung between two trees will help avoid tree damage. In tying horses to a picket line, keep compatible horses next to one another.

If you tie the horses too far from camp, you won't notice potential problems, such as the horses fighting, getting lost, or pulling loose. If they are tied too close to camp, the normal night noises of the horses can keep the camp awake. A good distance between campers and horses is between twenty and fifty yards.

Strings of horses that have been used and pastured together will tend to get along and stick together. Most novice camping parties will have horses that are not used to one another, and the horses will be less inclined to get along well and stay together. Once a horse is used regularly for horse camping, it will become a good "camp horse." It will accept the camp as home. While some outfitters successfully picket or tie two horses and allow the others to graze freely, this is a most risky practice.

Being set afoot by having your horses leave the country is one of the worst calamities that can befall a horse camper. Avoid losing horses regardless of the effort required to keep them in camp. Earl Hibbs says, "It's better to see their ribs than their tracks." Most show and pleasure horses suffer more from being overfed than from being underfed. If they lose some weight during a pack trip, it will do them more good than harm. The most agonized horse campers that I have ever encountered were those who had let their horses loose to graze, ignored them, and had them leave the area. In the autumn of 1940, I walked eight miles, from Cupboard Creek to the trailhead on the Selway River, to pick up my horses. That was the first and last time for me. Ever since, I have grazed horses and kept a sharp eye on them.

12. In Camp

MANY YEARS AGO, when the number of people using public land for camping was very small, some campers took pride in making a luxurious camp. No amount of camping time, effort, or native materials was spared to make the camp convenient and comfortable. Chairs, tables, and wash racks were made of logs and branches. Beds were laid upon thick mattresses of evergreen boughs. Poles were cut for tents, corrals, and saddle racks. The old-time camp often gave evidence of a lot of pioneering and woodcraft. Wood was plentiful because hardly anyone was using it.

Now, the conditions are very different. Many campers are using public lands, and if each one used even a single living tree, soon there wouldn't be any trees at all around popular camping areas. For this reason, use only dead timber that has been blown down to make your camp improvements—never use a living tree. Leave standing dead trees alone too, as they are the homes of pine squirrels, chipmunks, weasels, owls, bluebirds, and woodpeckers.

There is always someplace to go for day trips from the base camp. Plan the length of these trips so as to be in harmony with the condition of the riders. A pack trip is not an endurance ride. If you do not get to see everything you want to, come back to the same place again on another trip. Don't wear everyone out trying to do too much.

It's quite all right for people to stay in camp for the day, enjoying the solitude, the sights, and the sounds close by. The gourmet cook in the group might get more pleasure from staying in camp and creating a backcountry feast than spending the day in the saddle. In Kentucky, black oak is favored for cooking. In the northern Rockies, there is a lot of lodgepole pine, which has little commercial value, is short-lived, and is good for cooking, but not for overnight fires. Red fir (or Douglas-fir) bark makes a hot, steady fire, and a few pitchy chunks of Ponderosa pine will start the fire quickly.

Avoid cooking over an open wood fire. For beginners, the usual results of open-fire cooking are burned hands and black pots. About the only piece of cooking equipment suitable for the open fire is the Dutch oven. While being very heavy, the Dutch oven is often taken on horse camping trips. Learning to use one takes a little practice, but is well worth the effort. The usual problem is having too much heat on the bottom of the oven, and not enough on the top. Dutch ovens come in various sizes—I have a fourteen-inch oven that is four inches deep and works well for baking biscuits. I use a smaller (12-inch) and deeper (5-inch) oven for making beef stew with biscuits—a dish that provides meat, vegetables, and bread, all in one dish. My smallest Dutch oven (8-inch x 2½-inch) can accommodate biscuits for several people. The Dutch oven is helpful in breaking the usual routine of fried or boiled meats.

Grates are lightweight and will keep pots level, although the pots still get sooty over the open fire. On a wood stove or metal stove top placed over the fire, food can easily be kept warm on the edge of the cooking surface, while dishes that are being cooked can be set in the center. Charcoal is usually considered too heavy and bulky to carry on horse packing trips.

WATER

PEOPLE RAISED IN THE COUNTRY drinking out of creeks, springs, seeps, and cow tracks develop a tolerance for soil-borne organisms. A bug that would give a city-bred camper a bad case of diarrhea would usually not disturb an old cowpoke. The reason some people get a case of Montezuma's Revenge in Mexico is that they take on a strain of bacteria to which they have no immunity.

The purest water comes from springs, while that from creeks and lakes can contain organisms dangerous to your health. A protozoan called Giardia has now spread throughout North America and is of particular concern to campers. The protozoan is found in fast-flowing, clear, mountain streams that used to guarantee a drink of pure water. To be certain the Giardia is not present, boil water for ten minutes or treat it with iodine.

To use iodine, place four to eight grams of U.S.P. grade resublimed iodine (iodine crystals) in a clear, one-ounce glass bottle with a plastic, watertight, screw-on cap. Fill the glass with water. Shake well for a minute, and let the suspended crystals settle. Pour five capfuls (12½ cc) of the solution into a quart of water. The water is safe to drink after fifteen minutes. Use more capfuls for colder water.

The incubation period for Giardia cysts is, fortunately, from twelve to fifteen days, which means it doesn't affect most people until they are at home. Unfortunately, they often don't suspect what caused their problem. Giardiasis is characterized by diarrhea, nausea, cramps, loss of appetite, and a low-grade fever.

CLEAN CAMP

PRESENT-DAY CAMPERS place more emphasis on seeing and enjoying the countryside than they do on building a super-convenient and comfortable camp. In camp, the objective is to make a minimum impact on the environment. Even though you live in camp for several days, do as little as possible to your surroundings. If things are not torn up, and if the site is left as you found it, you will leave it in its natural state when you pack out.

If a ditch was dug for drainage, fill it up before leaving. Cover the latrine back up. Scatter the rocks collected for the fire ring, and if the horse droppings were piled up, scatter them too.

For a large party staying at the same location for several days, build a temporary outhouse using a manty or two. Construct a makeshift stool from a smooth pole lashed between two trees, and dig the pit about one foot deep. Refill the pit before the party leaves. Keep the latrine at least two hundred feet from the water supply and the campsite.

Small parties staying for a short time should dig a shovel full of soil about six inches deep, which will be used as a toilet, and then replace the soil. No one will know you have been there if you don't leave uncovered stool or used toilet paper on top of the ground. That is both unsanitary and unsightly.

Camping should be a restful and happy occasion. Being cranky or short-tempered is only appropriate when dealing with litter. If someone drops litter and does not immediately pick it up, make him feel as undeserving as possible. Small litter is still litter. Gum wrappers are just as offensive as empty cigarette packs and beer cans.

A bear hunting guest, Bob Harney, and I were riding back to the ranch after an unsuccessful day with the hounds. In recounting the incident later to friends, Bob said, "I peeled the cellophane off a little piece of hard candy, put the candy in my mouth, and tossed the cellophane—two inches wide and perfectly clear—on the ground. George stopped his horse, got off, and picked it up. I got the message. He didn't have to say a word."

People go to the backcountry to get away from all traces of civilization. A littered trail and littered campsite degrade the experience. People should not only take care to pick up their own litter, they should also be quick to pick up any other litter they see.

Litter begets litter. If junk is allowed to accumulate, the unfeeling and lazy will say, "No one else bothers to pick up litter, why should I?" On the other hand, if the country is perfectly clean, even the most callous slobs are reluctant to litter.

Horse campers are better equipped to carry out litter than are hikers because their horses are doing the work. In addition to packing out his own litter, a horse camper should pack out any other litter that can be found. It used to be that campers would dig a pit and bury their litter. It has been discovered that bears and other animals will often dig it up and scatter it about.

Tin cans should be flattened, and plastic and styrofoam crushed before being packed out. Burn paper and cardboard, but not plastics, which only melt and leave a littered fire pit. Burn any waste food such as bones, so that the odors won't attract bears and smell up the camp. Use a plastic bag inside a burlap sack for the camp garbage can. Tell everyone in the camp what the bag is for and where it is.

Everyone is part owner of the public land. It should be treated with the same pride and concern as your own front yard.

BEDDING DOWN

RESTFUL NIGHTS ARE A REQUISITE for exhilarating days. How restful they are will depend in part upon where you choose to bed down. The tent should be pitched in a well-drained and level place that has been cleared of rocks and sticks.

If there is a drainage problem, you can dig a ditch around the uphill side of the tent. Because most modern tents have their own floor, this is not as necessary as it once was. If the bed area slopes, place rolled-up clothing along the low side of the air mattress or foam pad. A folded, down jacket often takes the place of a pillow.

While I have never packed a pillow for myself, I have packed them for guests who felt they were essential to sound sleep.

You can tell the experienced campers by the way they take their clothes off before getting into their sleeping bags. People who have only lived in centrally heated houses will take their shirts off first. Anyone used to the outdoors, however, will start with their boots first, and then their pants. The shirts are only removed after getting into the sleeping bag. The hat comes off last.

Sweet dreams.

MORNING

ORNINGS CAN BE A BIT frosty. Put on your hat first, then inch out of your bag and pull on a shirt and jacket. Finally, crawl out and put on your socks, pants, and boots.

The first job of the first person up is to check on the horses. Then, if a horse is loose, tangled up, or otherwise in trouble, it can be taken care of.

The next step is to build a fire and put some water on to heat. There are always a few people in each party who have a negative attitude until they drink their first cup of coffee or some other hot drink.

If horse feed has been packed in, one or two people can feed the horses while others cook breakfast. If the horses are to be grazed, that can be done after breakfast while the camp is being cleaned up. One of the non-cooks can hustle water and fuel (if firewood needs to be gathered).

Food should be stored in a cool place during the day. If bears are present in the vicinity, keep foods that attract bears, such as bacon, peanut butter, jam, honey, and fruit, in a grub box. Throw a rope over a tree limb and hang the grub box at least fifteen feet above the ground. Hang it from a small tree, only four or five inches in diameter, which the bears will not be able to climb.

GRAZING

WHILE A VOLUNTEER is doing dishes, other members of the party can graze the horses. Each person going along should saddle and bridle a riding horse. If the horses are easy to drive and will stay together in a band, the remaining horses can be turned loose and driven to the grazing area. Horses that have not been horse camping before should be led to the grazing. If polypropylene lead ropes are used, they can be dragged by the horses—this will discourage any roaming tendencies. Hobble the three or four most frisky horses and the string will be less inclined to roam.

Upon arrival at the grazing area, the riders can pull the bridles off their horses, loop them over the horn, and tie them to the front saddle strings. A lead rope or hobbles can then be applied. Don't let the horses wander too far because they might decide they want to roll, and that will damage the saddles.

If the saddle horses seem particularly restless, keep a hand on the lead rope and don't depend upon hobbles. If a horse is spooked, it can cover some ground in spite of its hobbles. After a few days at the same campsite, the horses will become accustomed to their grazing and tie-up areas.

When the horses have grazed for several hours, they can be returned to camp and tied up. Don't drive a horse that is dragging its lead rope. Either lead it, or take off the rope. As soon as the horses get to camp, catch them and tie them up. With a handful of oats, bribe the horses that are difficult to catch. If that doesn't work, make a temporary rope corral and drive the horses into it. In the corral, they can be cornered and caught.

If the horses are ridden during the day, they can be grazed again in the evening. They should be watered each time they are grazed or fed. Avoid grazing in very steep country and in wet, boggy areas where the horses will sink into the mud, leaving deep holes at each step. Graze only twenty-five percent of the grass if it is early in the season. Mature grass is not damaged by heavy grazing.

When horses stop eating and start roaming around, they have had enough. Grazing them twice a day for a short period is better than grazing them once a day for long period.

ENTERTAINMENT

PACK TRIPS ARE TAKEN for escape, relaxation, and enjoyment. For a good fisherman, a little fishing will supply both food and entertainment. In the mountains, there is always the appeal of looking over the next ridge or into the next canyon. Going into new country is one of the strongest yearnings of horse campers.

You might be able to poke around in an old mining camp or explore the remains of an ancient trapper's cabin. If photographers can figure out where the game feeds, or where it beds down during the day, it is possible to be at the right place at the right time to take some unique wildlife pictures. Rock hounds can search for unusual stones, and hopeful prospectors can try a little gold panning.

When I packed Lew Portnoy, the photographer for this book, into the Seven Devils in Idaho, we rode to a different place each day. One day we rode to Three Creeks Point and had a breathtaking view of the Hells Canyon. On another day we rode to Dry Diggins Lookout and found a friendly attendant who told us how she managed her lookout responsibilities. One of her chores was carrying her water up from Bernard Lake, located a half-mile north and several hundred feet below the lookout.

Along the Snake River Trail near the Seven Devils are several sets of Indian pictographs on basalt walls. All we can do is speculate on their

meaning, as not even present day Indians can interpret them. When the high water recedes after the spring runoff, interesting artifacts from early Indian and white settlements are revealed.

On a trail ride in Kentucky, I learned to identify most of the native species of hardwoods. Seeing the remains of a moonshiner's still and an 1830 iron-smelting furnace were highlights of that ride.

The evening campfire is a part of the Old West that is still with us today. In the old days, mountain men, prospectors, cowboys, hunters, and outfitters sat around the fire, told stories, and sang. This is still one of the most enjoyable traditions of horse camping.

STRIKING CAMP

IF YOUR PARTY PLANS to pack out and drive home in one day, organize your gear the evening before. Things tend to get scattered around at the base camp, and it might take some time to gather your gear together.

After an early rising, eat breakfast, make lunch, and pack your personal gear before you take down the tents. This will give the tents a chance to dry before they are packed up.

While one or two of you graze or feed the horses, the rest can strike the camp and cargo packs. Each camper should bring his gear to a clean and level central location where it can be cargoed. After feeding the horses, saddle them. Do this some time before they are to be packed or ridden so that the saddle blankets have time to warm up and the horses have time to relax. They can be properly cinched when the time comes to leave.

If tent poles have been used, lean them against a tree where they will keep clean and will not rot. After the cargoing is well underway, make a thorough search of the entire camp area and beyond. Look around all trees, logs, and rocks to make certain that nothing is left behind. Check for things that might have fallen off a log or rock and have become camouflaged. There should be no litter left in the camp, in the horse tie-up area, or elsewhere. Smooth out areas that the horses have pawed, and leave the whole camp in better condition than when you found it. Use generous amounts of water to kill the fire.

As the packs are cargoed, those that weigh the same should be paired in preparation for loading. When most of the gear is cargoed, the gentlest of the packhorses can be led in, packed, and tied where it will be handy to hook up. The green horses should be packed last with non-rattling, indestructible cargo, such as tents and sleeping bags. When the last horse is packed, canvass the area looking for forgotten items, then hook up the horses and move out. Leave only tracks and take only memories from your wilderness experience.

PHOTOGRAPHER'S NOTES

TAKING PHOTOGRAPHS of and around horses is a joy. The scenic possibilities in the backcountry are endless. The only complication is dust. Unless you are first in line, the dust kicked up by the rest of the party will settle on your camera if you have it around your neck or in the open. I took care of this problem by keeping my cameras in a small, zipped-up backpack hung on the saddle in place of a saddlebag. The traditional saddlebag doesn't provide much protection because it is only closed with flaps. Any equipment that I wasn't intending to use as I rode along I would wrap in plastic bags and close with rubber bands.

Travel light to increase your mobility. Zoom lenses provide flexibility. Try to take photographs in the soft light of the early morning and late afternoon. Don't be a nuisance to your companions. Take lots of beautiful pictures.

I would like to thank George Hatley for an educational and enjoyable trip, and for the use of a wonderfully efficient Appaloosa whose consistent great performance made the photography so easy. Kris Portnoy cared for my horse in order that I could care for the cameras. All members of the group made photographing easy with their good nature and patience. Lois Constantz and David McCarthy are appreciated for the efforts in making the black and white prints. And finally, I would like to thank Juli Thorson for her energy and coordination in bringing about the trip.

Lewis Portnoy

PHOTO CREDITS

All photographs in this book are by Lewis Portnoy except the following:

page 12 (bottom), Ed Sala
page 24–25 (mules), Juli Thorson
page 25 (llama), stock photo
page 26, Ed Sala
page 28, Ed Sala
page 37, stock photos
page 42, Ed Sala
page 44, stock photo
page 54, stock photo
page 55, stock photo
page 62, stock photo
page 64, stock photo
page 71, stock photo
page 72, stock photo
page 73, Ed Sala
page 76, Ed Sala
page 78, Ed Sala
page 100, stock photos
page 105, stock photo
page 108, stock photo
page 111, stock photo

RESOURCES

ASSOCIATIONS

Alaska Professional Hunters Association,
www.alaskaprohunter.org

American Forests, www.americanforests.org

Arizona Game and Fish Department,
www.gf.state.az.us

California Department of Fish and Game,
www.dfg.ca.gov

Colorado Outfitters, www.colorado-outfitters.com

Horse & Mule Trail Guide USA,
www.horseandmuletrails.com

HorseCity, www.horsecity.com/trail_finder

Idaho Outfitters and Guides Association, www.ioga.org

Montana Outfitters and Guides Association,
www.montanaoutfitters.org

Nevada Department of Wildlife, www.ndow.org

New Mexico Council of Outfitters and Guides,
www.nmoutfitters.com

North American Trail Ride Conference, www.natrc.org

Ontario Trail Riders Association, www.otra.ca

Oregon Guides and Packers Association, www.ogpa.org

Trail Riders of the Canadian Rockies,
www.trail-rides.ca

Trail Town USA, www.trailtownusa.com

Utah Guides and Outfitters Association,
www.utahguidesandoutfitter.com

Washington Outfitters and Guides Association,
www.woga.org

Wyoming Outfitters and Guides Association,
www.wyoga.org

BREED ORGANIZATIONS

The breed organizations listed below have trail riding
programs and provide support services for trail riders.

American Morgan Horse Association,
www.morganhorse.com

American Paint Horse Association, www.apha.com

American Pinto Horse Association, www.pinto.org

American Quarter Horse Association, www.aqha.com

Appaloosa Horse Association, www.appaloosa.com

Arabian Horse Association, www.arabianhorses.org

Missouri Fox Trotting Horse Breed Association,
www.mfthba.com

American Donkey and Mule Society,
www.lovelongears.com

Norwegian Fjord Horse Registry, www.nfhr.com

Tennessee Walking Horse Breeders' and Exhibitor's
Association, www.twhbea.com

HORSE PUBLICATIONS

Horse & Rider, www.horseandrider.com

Horse Illustrated, www.horsechannel.com

Trail Blazer, www.trailblazermagazine.us

The Trail Rider, www.myhorse.com

Western Horseman, www.westernhorseman.com

EQUIPMENT

Custom Packrigging, www.custompackrigging.com

Dale Pack Station, www.deckerpacksaddles.com

Mountain Horse Inc.,
www.montanamountainhorse.com

Ralide Inc., www.ralide.com

Ralph Shimon Company, www.ralphshimon.com

Ray Holes Leather Care Products,
www.rayholesleathercare.com

Ray Holes Saddle Company, 213 W Main St,
Grangeville, ID 83530, 208-983-1460

TRAIL RIDES

Chief Joseph Appaloosa Trail Ride, www.appaloosa.
com/trail/2009TrailRides.htm#joseph

Gordon's Guide, horse-pack-trips.gordonsguide.com

Sheltowee (Daniel Boone) Appaloosa Trail Ride, www.
appaloosa.com/trail/2009TrailRides.htm#sheltowee